THE BOOK ON MORTGAGE PLANNING

BY

LEON L. MORRIS, RFC, CLU, CHFC, CME, RMP, FFSI

Phone 678.388.7823 • Fax 770.517.2864

THE BOOK ON MORTGAGE PLANNING

About The Author

Leon L. Morris, RFC, CLU, ChFC, CME, RMP, FFSI

Leon Morris started his financial services career in 1983 as an insurance agent in Florida. Since then, Leon has worked in the insurance and financial services industry as a Special Agent, Sales Manager, General Agent, Registered Representative, Mortgage Broker and Registered Investment Adviser. Leon also worked for a number of years as a Senior Associate, (Technical Specialist & Product Manager) for the Life Office Management Association (LOMA). During his employment with LOMA, Leon was directly responsible for product development in the Association's Management Resources Division with a focus on equity products, annuities, broker-dealer operations and pensions.

Leon was engaged in original research, creating, organizing, promoting and conducting technical training seminars and workshops, and managing executive level committee meetings throughout the United States and Canada. Leon has been President & CEO of Morris Capital Management (MCM) since he founded the company in June of 1995. MCM has operated as a Georgia Residential Mortgage Licensee, a Florida Licensed Mortgage Brokerage Business, and a Registered Investment Adviser. Leon is the Executive Director of the Mortgage Institute for Financial Services Professionals, Inc. (MIFSP).

Leon completed his undergraduate degree with an interdisciplinary double major concentration in economics and government from the College of Social Sciences at Florida State University in 1985. He received designations as a Chartered Life Underwriter (CLU) and Chartered Financial Consultant (ChFC) from the American College in 1991 and 1993, respectively. Leon received the Associate, Customer Service (ACS) designation from LOMA with honors in the first class of designees in 1992 and LOMA's Fellow, Financial

Services Institute (FFSI) in 2005. He also was awarded LOMA's Associate, Life Management Institute (ALMI) in 2006. Leon received the Certified Mortgage Evaluator (CME) designation and Residential Mortgage Planner® (RMP®) designation in 2003 from the Mortgage Institute for Financial Services Professionals, Inc.

Leon is a Registered Financial Consultant (RFC) and held the National Association of Securities Dealers (NASD) Series 6, 7, and North American Securities Administrators (NASA) Series 63, and 65. He has held Georgia licenses for life, health and variable products. He also holds a Florida and Georgia mortgage broker's license. Leon is the author of the books *Managing Your Mortgage To Financial Independence* and *The ABCs of Mortgage Based Financial Planning*. Leon currently resides in the metro Atlanta area with his wife of twenty-one years and their two children.

DEDICATION

This book is dedicated to all financial services professionals who are concerned about the general welfare of their clients, homeowners and consumers such that they are willing to dedicate time and spirit to the continued exploration of ways to serve them better.

ACKNOWLEDGEMENTS

Thank you to my wife and children for their love and support during the writing of this book. Thank you to my friends and supporters for lending at least one ear as I spoke almost endlessly while thinking through the essence of my message. Thank you to all those in industry and academia who have given thought to the plight of the mortgagor.

PREFACE

Mortgage planning is a relatively new phenomenon that's sweeping the nation. However, at this point, there are no set criteria for what constitutes "mortgage planning". Being that it's still in its infancy, how mortgage planning develops and how it's practiced determines whether it has enough support and sustenance to flourish as a financial specialty.

No doubt there is a vast lack of knowledge when it comes to mortgages and investing (selection, strategy, evaluation and management) at the individual level, but more often than not when it comes to mortgages, the focus is on qualifying rather than planning. However, a mortgage no longer comes in just a plain vanilla thirty-year fixed rate package. It now comes with frills and options that weren't available a few years ago. Also, mortgage decisions impact other long-term and short-term financial goals; therefore, developing a strategy, whether you want plain vanilla or the frills and options, is not only good financial thinking it is just good common sense.

The sometimes hurried pace of mortgage origination does not lend itself to the thoughtful process of planning beyond the short-term goal of loan approval. However, being that it's expected to last longer than one year, a mortgage is a long-term debt, and it's the long-term nature of mortgages that makes it tremendously beneficial to establish mortgage related goals, strategies and action steps. Housing is the largest cost the average consumer has; therefore, when it comes to discussions of the best ways to minimize those costs and maximize the benefits of true homeownership, mortgage planning should be the place to start.

Consumer's faith in saving may be hampered by believing that they have to run with the bulls in the stock market in order to achieve wealth and financial freedom and if they don't have enough money to run with the bulls, they're relegated to the sidelines and so are their dreams of financial freedom. One of the best things about mortgage planning is that it's for all mortgagors regardless of whether they hear a jingle in their pockets or the crumbling of dollar bills.

The purpose of this book is to explain the basics of mortgage planning and to promote the processes that will enable mortgage planning to continue to grow and flourish as a financial specialty.

Table of Contents

Chapter 1

Mortgage Planning - Filling A Growing Need

"In the following pages I offer nothing more than simple facts, plain arguments, and common sense and have no other preliminaries to settle with the reader, than that he will divest himself of prejudice and prepossession, and suffer his reason and his feelings to determine for themselves that he will put on, or rather that he will not put off, the true character of a man, and generously enlarge his views beyond the present day."

Common Sense by Thomas Paine
(February 14, 1776)

The complexity and sophistication of mortgage loan programs have grown tremendously since the 1930s and 1940s. When there was little variation in mortgage options and few choices in providers, consumers were at risk of making fewer mistakes due to loan program selection, strategy implementation, evaluation, and management. However, as the mortgage industry develops more and more loan programs and products, the details and subtle variations of these programs, and cost differences, along with the increase in the selection and the types of loan originators, and the continuous lack of objective mortgage advice make it ever more difficult for consumers to make choices that are truly right for them. With over 100 million households, mortgage planning can easily become a $50 billion dollar industry if each of these households utilized the services of a mortgage planner at an average cost of just $500 per year. Mortgage planning can save mortgagors tens of thousands of dollars in costly mistakes and unnecessary risk taking, making it a good deal at just about any price.

On May 24, 2006, the Consumer Federation of America (CFA) issued a press release summarizing the results of research findings that appeared in a CFA released study, *Exotic or Toxic? An Examination of the Non-Traditional Mortgage Market for Consumers and Lenders,* whereby CFA analyzed certain borrower and loan characteristics of more than 100,000 mortgages originated between January and October 2005. CFA stated that their data offers one of the first opportunities to examine characteristics of non-traditional mortgage borrowers. Patrick Woodall, CFA's Senior Researcher stated that "Non-traditional mortgages are more complex than your parents' home loan, and some highly leveraged or unsophisticated consumers could end up learning that the mortgage that helped them buy their home was a ticking time bomb that destroyed their finances for years." CFA's report is said to examine the implications of the rapid rise of non-traditional mortgages and how these products pose additional risks for borrowers. CFA stated "...non-traditional mortgage products may benefit certain consumers, but pose more risks than benefits for many others. There are indications that many borrowers do not fully understand that these mortgages expose borrowers to potentially sharp increases in borrowing costs. Federal

Regulators recently urged lenders to provide more comprehensive information to borrowers. However, given the array and complexity of many of the new products being offered, improved disclosures may not be enough. The plain fact is that deferred payment mortgage products simply may not be appropriate for all borrowers who receive them and therefore, a threat to homeownership sustainability. Suitability standards that protect borrowers from getting inappropriate mortgage products would be one solution CFA believes is worth considering."[1]

Even if non-traditional loans aren't under consideration, mortgage planning helps homeowners structure financing and refinancing decisions to take advantage of positive changes in credit, rates and terms, among other things, to effectively lower their total cost of home financing over time until the mortgage is retired. Just as importantly, if not more so, mortgage planning is beneficial to retirement planning for homeowners who are concerned about matching post retirement income with retirement expense levels, and beneficial to any mortgagor seeking a no cost low risk way to move closer to financial freedom.

Although there are numerous free pamphlets and websites meant to provide guidance in mortgage selection, refinancing and other mortgage related decisions, even the savviest do-it-yourselfer may come up short when it comes to understanding how to apply these tips on an individual level. The general hard and fast rules of thumb don't always apply on an individual basis and most likely will not result in the best answer when applied on that level. Mortgage planning is a personal service that avoids the snags of going from the general to the specific.

The sheer magnitude of the dollars involved makes home financing decisions one of the most significant money management decisions consumers have to make. Yet they are left to their own devices when it comes to gathering and deciphering mortgage information and they are looking for a better way. *The Book On Mortgage Planning* is the guide for the practitioner who wants to help them find it.

What You'll Find In *The Book On Mortgage Planning*

Generally, there is a lack of awareness and understanding as to what a mortgage planner is, what a mortgage planner does, and what a mortgage planner should be. Each chapter in this book paves the way for the reader to gain a clearer understanding of mortgage planning and the job analysis techniques that were employed in determining and describing the role of a mortgage planner. Chapter 1 tells the reader how and by what means a mortgage planner can personally contribute to this ongoing analysis and what a mortgage planner can do to raise the standards of practice and acceptance of the mortgage planning professional by state & federal regulators and the consuming public alike.

In Chapter 2, the reader learns about the types of relationships that can lead to more mortgage planning opportunities, the significance of the relationships the practitioner has with a client, and about related coordination and functional relationships. In Chapter 3, the reader is introduced to the kinds of data that must be gathered for the mortgage planning engagement, the significance of the data, what the practitioner can reasonably expect to draw from the data, managing a client's expectations based on the data gathered, and where and how to start the data gathering process.

Chapter 4 introduces appropriate benchmarks, earmarks and hallmarks in mortgage planning, the limits to mortgage planning and the mortgage plan. Chapter 5 answers the question of what to do with the data you've got and the social, legal, and professional constraints that mortgage planners face, along with the issue of accountability and what to do if you fall short.

Chapter 6 gets into mortgage plan development and how mortgage planners communicate their findings with clients (telling clients not only what they want to know, but also what they need to know in order to make intelligent mortgage and financial decisions). Chapter 7 deals with plan implementation and the role and responsibilities of the mortgage planner. Chapter 8 focuses on monitoring the mortgage, the importance of monitoring and of looking backward as well as forward to access the client's progress.

Chapter 9 presents a mortgage theory that supports mortgage planning and shows sound reasoning behind the concept. In Chapter 10, the steps of the process of mortgage planning are outlined in detail creating a common gauge of what mortgage planning is all about.

What Has Lead To An Interest In Mortgage Planning?

Interest in the concept of "mortgage planning" by business and consumers is a manifestation of the precarious position many consumers find themselves in 2006. The decisions made in purchasing, maintaining and refinancing a home have long-term financial consequences and consumers are vulnerable in deciphering the immediate impact of these decisions, not to mention how these decisions will, can, and do impact their abilities to fulfill other future financial responsibilities and goals. For the most part, when it comes to mortgages, consumers have been lead to focus on meeting underwriting guidelines in what for some is an arduous quest and for others almost quick or instant loan approval. However, consumers are finding that hearing the words "you're approved" do not always lead to a happy ending.

Likely because of the sophistication of some loan programs and the increase in home equity consumers are starting to realize that they need a mortgage professional with a special awareness and competence who is willing to see beyond the bright lights of the underwriting guidelines to the immediate, short-term and long-term financial goals of the client and who is able to show them how to make mortgage decisions that will advance rather than sink those goals. Consumers are seeing a need to take a more holistic or coordinated and proactive approach to considering the impacts of their mortgage decisions on meeting their major life's goals and objectives. Without proper mortgage planning a need goes unmet, whether it's for a second opinion from a competent sounding board, professional insight as to how to set financial priorities including the mortgage, or for an objective professional perspective on individual mortgage choices, mortgage options and related items that should be given proper consideration.

The Emerging Need for Mortgage Planning

As will be discussed throughout the book, mortgage planning creates a unique opportunity for the mortgage professional to move to the forefront on the consumers' financial planning agenda. Everyday thousands of people reach adulthood and are faced with the decision of where to live and whether they are going to buy or rent their next home. This provides daily opportunities to have positive mortgage planning interaction and to begin building a long-term professional relationship with large numbers of homebuyers and those who want to become homebuyers.

With over 30% of the average consumer's income going towards housing and 66% of all households being owner occupied households, it shouldn't be surprising that the largest single asset most Americans believe they have is their home. (Typically the largest single asset is actually time and how it's spent impacts their earning capacity, another intangible asset.) Being that housing is the largest single expense[2] and the home is the biggest physical asset most consumers have, attention to the existence or planned existence of the mortgage should not be overlooked. The 2002 Consumer Expenditure Survey showed that housing expenses averaged 32.7% of income before taxes for homeowners and 34.5% of income for renters. The survey also showed that on average 19.1% of gross income for both homeowners and renters went to cover transportation expenses. The 2006 annual report, *The State of the Nation's Housing,* released by the Joint Center for Housing Studies of Harvard University, reported that one in three American households now spends more than 30 percent of income on housing, and one in seven spends more than 50 percent.[3]

Average Annual Expenditures

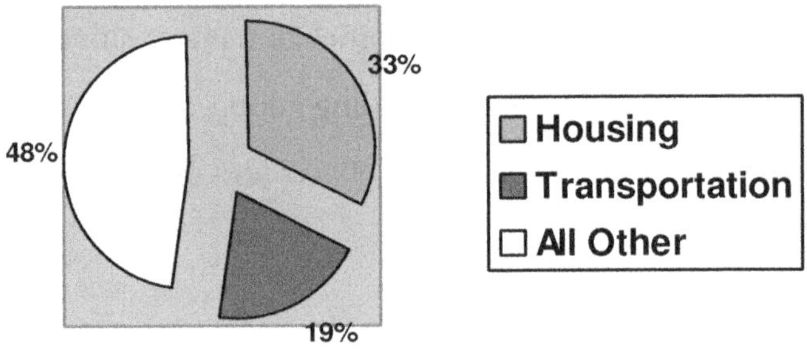

Source: Consumer Expenditure Survey, 2002, U.S. Department of Labor, Bureau of Labor Statistics

Housing expenses represent such a significant portion of the average consumers' outflow of cash that just focusing on managing this aspect of the consumers' finances will do far more for far more people than we may presently realize. Can planning by focusing on the biggest debt and most valuable physical asset bring about much needed financial improvement? Can expanding the numbers of practitioners who acquire the knowledge to bring about this change make financial independence a reality for more people much sooner? The answers to these questions are yes and yes.

Residential property values have increased significantly in many areas throughout the country over the past ten years resulting in home equity growth, in many cases, that is beyond the wildest expectations of the homeowner. In these situations, deciding what to do with home equity may cause the homeowner to feel like it's a gamble: Should I let it ride and not touch it? Should I cash it in by selling my home? Or should I leverage it to pay off other debts or liquefy it for other purposes? These are not questions to be taken lightly and the answers may not always be as simple as one might think. However, mortgage planning can help provide objective and unbiased answers to these types of questions.

In a speech at the 2006 Annual Meeting of the Certified Financial Planner Board of Standards, Inc. on August 4, 2006, Mary Schapiro, then Vice Chairman, NASD President, Regulatory Policy & Oversight stated that Americans are "dis-saving" as spending exceeds income, "…A key factor—and a paradoxical one, at that—is the so-called wealth effect, whereby people save less as they see their net worth growing. And, my goodness, how our net worth has increased over the last couple of decades as the value of our homes that provide the roofs over our heads has itself gone through the roof. But what has occurred is a rash of home mortgage refinancing so that owners can take equity out of their houses and spend it. Baby-boomers, are piling up debt—drawing on home-equity lines of credit, running up balances on their credit cards—at alarming rates, all to finance current consumption at the expense of long-term savings…[4]

Mortgage planning brings rational thought to this type of uncontrolled spending and brings focus and hope to millions of middle income Americans who spend as if financial independence is too far out of reach. Consumers may feel that small amounts of discretionary income are not worth the effort of saving, however, through mortgage planning they can be shown how even small amounts can lead directly to financial freedom.

Can Mortgage Planning Survive Let Alone Thrive?

Presently mortgage planning can mean anything from a dressed up name for mortgage origination to persuading a homeowner to borrow home equity to invest in risk intensive financial products in hopes of earning a higher return to developing a long-term mortgage strategy tailor made for each individual that is monitored by a Qualified

Mortgage Planner™ (QMP) or Mortgagor Financial Representative™ professional. Can mortgage planning survive with such diversity in meaning? Well the answer is up to the practitioners of mortgage planning.

Mortgage planning has to be associated with high ethical standards and competent practitioners in order to survive and thrive as a financial services specialty, and there has to be basic uniformity and understanding of the underlying processes, and concepts unique to mortgage planning. It is up to mortgage planners to recognize the need for competence and ethical standards, to set and accept those standards, and to help educate or expose those who abuse the standards or use their influence on consumers for selfish gains.

Use of standardized processes and concepts enable mortgage planners not only to distinguish themselves in the market place, but also helps manage consumer expectations and starts all mortgage planning practitioners on the same page. In other words, it means that at a minimum in mortgage planning certain procedures, processes, and practices are followed that result in providing certain basic information to the client.

On the contrary, can mortgage planning be adequately defined if there are wide variations in the procedures, processes, practices and aims of mortgage planning? If there is no uniformity in these areas, how will practitioners and their clients know where (and how) to start the mortgage planning engagement, who and what's involved, what differentiates mortgage planning from any other form of financial planning or when the engagement is over?

The answer to the last question is easy for those who use mortgage planning to dress up mortgage origination. For them, the short answer is that mortgage planning starts with a mortgage application and ends with funding. Should mortgage planning be more than a gimmick to sell loans? Should practitioners expect to provide more and should consumers expect to receive more?

In contrast to the emerging field of mortgage planning, traditional professionals in medicine, theology and law (the learned professions) are generally required to complete a certification or licensing process that requires completion of a comprehensive (extensive and broad) training and educational program where they are required to study, learn and master a specialized field of knowledge, demonstrate their understanding and ability to apply their specialized knowledge by passing an examination(s) or meeting some experience (internship, externship or residency) requirement after "professing" to uphold or support a particular (professional) code of conduct or set of guidelines publicized by one or more professional associations.

Unlike some of the learned professions, mortgage planning doesn't have a two thousand year old history. However, the desire or motivation for getting into this profession is becoming more apparent everyday. While some emergent entities, organizations and software vendors under the guise or moniker of mortgage planning promote the idea that "not delivering mortgage planning services will cost you a small fortune and possibly a career that is respected at the level of a CPA and Financial Planner and promote the ability to crush your competition," crushing the competition is not what "mortgage planning" is about.

Mortgage planning is not a zero sum game. It does not call for an all for me and none for you attitude or stance. Does "crushing your competition" sound like your life's calling? As you ponder that question, there are at least two things you should consider:

- Elevating the status of mortgage planning to that enjoyed by CPAs or Financial Planners is a laudable goal.
- More likely than not, professionals compete for business based on service quality (business reputation-expertise & knowledge) and what he/she can do to assist the customer (demonstrated results). What profession has as its focus the desire to "crush" the competition?

Mortgage planning is all about the mortgagor, mortgagor risk identification, risk classification, full disclosure, and control and management of mortgage related decisions. Most homeowners simply aren't aware of or can't adequately measure the risks that they are exposed to, either because they haven't given it much, if any, thought or there hasn't been a commercial mechanism or service available due to insufficient profit and/or service motives that draw new entrants into the field. Mortgage planning creates both profit and service motives. With mortgage planning, homeowners in the present and even more so in the future, will be shown how to transfer risk, how to avoid risk, and how to be adequately compensated/rewarded for the risks they take. This creates a win-win situation not only for homeowners, but both product and service providers as innovation will lead to new products and services just like the growth of the personal computing market following the movement from mainframe computers to desktop, laptop and mobile computing.

Traditional financial plans and emergent mortgage plans are prone to estimation risk, interest rate risk, timing risk, and management risk, among other things. (Several other forms of risk are discussed in Chapter 5.) The estimates used in traditional financial plans often reflect many factors that are outside the homeowner's and financial planner's control. Consequently, estimates of the amount of risk required in order to achieve a targeted financial goal maybe and often is miscalculated.

For example, one form of timing risk results from assumptions that certain rates of return will be achieved by a certain time. If the timing is off, the rate of return may not have been achieved when the homeowner needs it, if it's achieved at all. If the date or rate of return is off, it may mean the difference between early retirement, a comfortable retirement and a delayed retirement.

Mortgage planning focuses on the positive - taking positive action and movement toward the achievement of the mortgagor's financial goals, objectives, and outcomes - all the while recognizing the client's current and anticipated position, cycle of life, and how the homeowner identifies and manages both their money and their risks. Mortgage planning goes beyond general financial planning as it's practiced today and it addresses a basic question raised by the Certified Financial Planning Board of Standards & Practices: Is there a need for advanced or specialty education and designations?

The concept of mortgage planning creates great opportunities to provide positive results. It also creates opportunities for the professional growth and development of mortgage originators and others beyond the mortgage transaction; and it creates great opportunities for consumers and mortgagors to connect (interconnect & relate) the mortgage to other aspects of their financial existence. To date mortgages are another piecemeal financial decision and most people still make due without the benefits of an objective financial plan.

According to researchers at Ohio State University, based on the 1998 Survey of Consumer Finances, over one-fifth (21.2%) of households use financial planners. A much smaller portion (2.7%) gets advice from financial planners on only credit or borrowing.[5] The average consumer's financial existence is just a hodgepodge of disconnected piecemeal decisions. For a large number of consumers and mortgagors, mortgage planning may be the only financial plan developed for any aspect of their financial future. Mortgage planning provides a natural bridge between a homeowner's current financial positions (where they are today) and where they want to be tomorrow or in the distant future.

By taking mortgage planning beyond a mortgage transaction and by giving time and attention to understanding the mortgagor's objectives behind the mortgage as well as to considering the motivations behind those objectives, coupled with the knowledge of the underlying mortgage planning processes and concepts, practitioners can catapult what may have started out as a sales gimmick into a worthwhile financial specialty. Through mortgage planning, consumers and mortgagors can be lead through the maze of mortgage choices and its many pitfalls, and guided toward mortgage decisions that will help them reach their general financial goals. At a minimum, mortgage planning should help the consumer/mortgagor identify their goals and show them how to work toward achieving those goals while being made aware of all the major risks and options.

The long-term benefits of mortgage planning will be missed if it is solely thought of as a one-time <u>or</u> sales engagement. As long as the consumer/mortgagor has a home or desires to have a home, there is an ongoing need for mortgage planning. Once a plan is created, the plan should be monitored monthly or quarterly and updated as appropriate due to changes in circumstances, but no less often than annually in order to keep the consumer or mortgagor on course and to timely modify the plan due to changing family or financial circumstances or situations.

Defining Mortgage Planning

In reaching a common definition of mortgage planning, let's start by deciding whom we are trying to plan for and why.

- Should mortgage planning be concerned with planning for a primary residence, a secondary residence, and/or an investment property?
- Is mortgage planning to be used for an owner occupied property or an investment property?

The focus of the mortgage differs depending on the function of the property being mortgaged and the elements under consideration also change depending on the function of the property. For example, if the property is an investment property, the mortgagor is more focused on income potential and rate of return and how the investment property compares with other competing investment opportunities. If the property is a secondary residence, the client may have sufficient resources such that there is less concern about how mortgage decisions will affect other financial goals.

In establishing the mortgage on a primary residence as the target of mortgage planning, the variables under consideration are easier to distinguish and the path to goal achievement is clearer. When it comes to a primary residence, the mortgage planning engagement is jump-started when the consumer either wants to acquire a new mortgage, or a mortgagor wants to refinance an existing mortgage, re-evaluate an existing mortgage and/or move toward retiring an existing mortgage.

We've already established that mortgage planning is for the benefit of the consumer/mortgagor. We've also acknowledged that a residential mortgage represents a significant portion of most mortgagors' income. Being that housing preferences are driven by financial means as well as lifestyle choices and personality distinctions, these factors must also be taken into consideration in mortgage planning. Not to mention that the efficient allocation of resources and risk management is critical in assisting a consumer in planning for their goals.

Taking all of these factors into account yields the following definition of mortgage planning:

> **Mortgage Planning is a client focused goal oriented process of efficiently allocating and managing a mortgagor's resources and risks in a way that takes into account the mortgagor's lifestyle goals and objectives with due consideration given to the mortgagor's personality and socioeconomic environment to arrive at the most appropriate mortgage decision under the circumstances.**

Mortgage planning is all about creating a dialogue with a homeowner or prospective homeowner to collect facts about the client and then applying professional skill, knowledge, and professional objectiveness to improve the status of the homeowner/prospective homeowner while improving the practice and standing of personal mortgage planning. In its truest form, mortgage planning can do anything from improving the quality of service provided by mortgage originators and other financial services professionals to becoming a viable stand-alone profession impacting mortgage, retirement, savings and investment decision-making. The concept has phenomenal possibilities.

Hi, I'm A Mortgage Planner

Can it really be that simple? Well the simple answer is yes. It has become trendy to use the words "planner" or "planning" as bait to entice consumers to buy financial products including mortgages. Some tactics marketed to practitioners include "well-named" marketing credentials that are meant to convey a sense of knowledge and professionalism to the consumer. Catchy phrases and terminology using the words "planner" or "planning" tend to give a false impression of the benefits to consumers, but with all the confusion this causes who loses out in the long run?

Unlike doctors, lawyers or certified public accountants, there are no state sanctioned requirements for either financial planners or mortgage planners. There are no minimal educational requirements that one must fulfill before calling ones self or holding ones self out as either a financial planner or a mortgage planner.

Surprisingly official barriers to entry as a financial planner are very low. As simple as it sounds, it is a fact that anyone can call himself or herself a financial planner. In the field of financial planning, those who choose to practice financial planning generally employ or promote the financial planning process voluntarily. Because financial planning is generally recognized as a process, it stands to reason that by practicing the widely recognized (at least among practitioners) financial planning process one becomes a financial planner. The financial planning process will be discussed further in Chapter 10.

The financial planning industry is very fortunate in that members of the profession serve the public via a mechanism of self-regulation with no unnecessary government intervention, regulation, or layers, and without any of the other commonly associated costs of government intervention or licensing. Although legally it is clearly understood or common knowledge that if one engages in one or more of the related financial planning occupations, such as insurance sales agent, security, commodity or financial services sales agent (registered representative), real estate sales agent or broker, public accounting, or investment adviser, then you as the financial services professional would be regulated or subject to state or federal licensing requirements related to those fields. And while there are no restrictions, laws or regulations covering the financial planning process, there is also little regulation on the use of the title financial planner. Some well-credentialed financial planners may frown upon the latter point.

According to the Bureau of Labor Statistics, U.S. Department of Labor, *Occupational Outlook Handbook*, 2006-07 Edition, Loan Officers, on the internet http://www.bls.gov/oco/ocos018.htm there are an estimated 291,000 loan officers/mortgage originators within the United States, 90% of whom worked in commercial banks, credit unions, community banks, savings and loans, and related financial institutions. The largest trade association for mortgage brokers, the National Association of Mortgage Brokers, boasts a national membership of approximately 27,000 (http://www.namb.org). The Mortgage Bankers Association states that it has over 3,000 member companies and estimates that the industry employs more than 500,000 people in every community in the country (http://www.mbaa.org).

The *Occupational Outlook Handbook* states, "employment of loan officers is projected to increase more slowly than average for all occupations through 2014...the use of credit scoring has made the loan evaluation process much simpler than in the past and even unnecessary in some cases...in addition, the mortgage application process has become highly automated and standardized a simplification that has enabled online mortgage loan vendors to offer their services over the Internet."

There are some who refer to themselves generally as "mortgage planners". However, like some who may refer to themselves as "financial planners", more than likely these so called "mortgage planners" are not actually "mortgage planning" professionals. They generally use the label as a way of conveying knowledge, skills, abilities, and experience that they simply don't have, and their business operations may have no connection to any "planning" process or even more importantly any planning theory. Presently, the number of firms and individuals identified as "mortgage planners" makes mortgage planning a cottage industry (small scale, loosely organized) with most self-styled mortgage planners being involved in mortgage origination rather than offering mortgage planning on a stand alone basis. The *Occupational Outlook Handbook* indicates that the employment outlook for personal financial advisors is expected to grow faster than average for all occupations through 2014.

Extreme caution should be used when using a "mortgage planner" business model that includes crossing over into other financial sectors, such as investment planning, that maybe outside of your area of expertise. State and federal regulations come into play whenever investment advice is dispensed. These regulations include licensing requirements that you may be required to meet. If you are not an investment advisor or registered investment advisor, drawing analogies between residential mortgages and investment options may put you in violation of the Investment Advisors Act of 1940 and could cause you to have to be registered with your state securities regulator or at the federal level with the Securities & Exchange Commission. For example, suggesting that a homeowner obtain a mortgage to "pull out home equity" and invest the funds elsewhere because (as you claim) "home equity earns a zero rate of return" compared to other investment options could be viewed as crossing the line if you operate as a mortgage broker/originator and not an investment advisor. Investment advisors are considered fiduciaries and they must disclose any conflicts of interest.

Under the heading of "mortgage planning" a new trend exists whereby with the assistance of mortgage originators and financial representatives, homeowners are borrowing home equity to make investments in hopes of reaping a higher return than the rate paid on the mortgage loan. When it comes to integrating mortgages with investment strategies, there is great temptation and many hidden dangers for both the professional and the homeowner/mortgagor. Therefore, particularly in these instances, following an established uniform mortgage planning process and avoiding the urge to dispense advice in areas outside of your expertise are not only beneficial to the customer, but it could also keep the practitioner from testing the limits of their professional liability coverage. (This is covered in greater detail in Chapter 2.)

In addition to failing to meet the licensing requirements, it may be viewed as fraud or misrepresentation to solicit consumers through advertisements that implicitly or explicitly exaggerate your knowledge in areas that are beyond your expertise. If you are a mortgage originator, when offering mortgage planning, it's best to stick to mortgages. Leave the investment analogies to those who are properly licensed, registered or otherwise qualified to do so. With all that mortgage planning can rightfully do for consumers, there is no need to risk sanctions, fines, or imprisonment to find a flourishing market for mortgage planning.

In March 2004, the National Association of Securities Dealers (NASD) announced that it had taken separate enforcement actions against three securities brokers for making unsuitable recommendations to customers, urging them to purchase investments using proceeds obtained from cash-out home mortgage refinancing. NASD also issued an *Investor Alert* highlighting the dangers associated with mortgaging a home to fund investments. "A recommendation by a securities firm or a broker that an investor mortgage his home to buy securities raises all kinds of regulatory red flags", said Mary L. Schapiro, NASD's Vice Chairman. "NASD will always ask whether it is appropriate to recommend that you risk your home to seek investment returns."[6]

As mortgage planning progresses and develops into a recognized profession, consumers will be able to recognize the standards of the professional mortgage planner and will be able to differentiate between those who are truly qualified to provide mortgage planning services, from those who are co-opting the name in order to sell a mortgage or other financial products. Over the next eight years mortgage planning can become the fastest growing financial service and the fastest growing fee-for-service planning specialty in the country.

Therefore, what is a mortgage planner?

A Mortgage Planner is a professional that follows the mortgage planning process and recognizes the mortgage on a primary residence as part of a client's total portfolio and is capable, qualified and offers to provide mortgage planning services (actionable information) up to the evaluation level (the highest level on Bloom's Taxonomy) while maintaining high ethical standards by <u>not</u> promoting fraudulent or unethical mortgage practices.

Recognizing The Need For Mortgage Planning

Even with all of the free information available to homeowners, there's still no shortage of headlines and articles concerning the potential fallout and financial devastation to homeowners resulting from choosing mortgage products that can't be sustained over time or of ongoing homeowner confusion regarding what mortgage choices are best, when they're best, when they should be changed, or when they should be avoided altogether. Not to mention that homeowners are still left wondering how to balance their mortgage and lifestyle goals and risks against their short and long-term financial needs and goals, e.g. retirement.

Because they didn't know what was right for their particular situation or because they didn't know when or how to shift gears through the various mortgage programs, many homeowners are at this moment dangling from a cliff waiting for the impacts or aftershock of non-traditional loans or poor mortgage choices. Many more homeowners don't have a clue about the big picture view of their home and mortgage and what it means to view their mortgage as part of a larger portfolio.

While just about anyone is a candidate for mortgage planning, the ideal candidates are individuals, families, prospective homeowners and homeowners who are concerned about their own and their household's well being, dignity and financial security and who receive 85% or more of their annual income from earned income and whose individual earned income is equal to or less than the Social Security Contribution and Benefit Base ($94,200 for 2006). This target market covers approximately 85% of American households from the standpoint of income with no actual upper limit. These households relate well to goal actualization. And owning a home remains a primary goal for tens of millions of Americans.

According to a National Association of Realtors survey, the *2005 National Association of Realtors Profile of Home Buyers and Sellers*, "married couples make up the largest share of the housing market, accounting for 61 percent of transactions. Single women purchase 21 percent of homes while single men account for 9 percent. Unmarried couples were 7 percent of the market, and 2 percent were listed as other."[7] Additionally, according to National Association of Realtors, the median home price on an existing home went from $180, 200 in 2003 to $228, 500 by May 2006. That's an increase of 26.8%.[8]

Foreclosures remain at all time highs for many states including California, Colorado, Nevada, and Texas[9]; meanwhile the price of existing homes declined nationally for the first time in 11 years in August, 2006. The National Association of Realtors® (NAR) reported that the median price for existing single-family homes nationwide slipped 1.7% from last August 2005, which was the first such decline since April 1995. This was reported to be the second-biggest decline in the 38 years the Realtors have gathered sales data[10].

Some publicly available information warns consumers to stay away from nontraditional mortgages other information tells them that a nontraditional mortgage maybe exactly what's needed to get into the home of their dreams. Although there is an abundance of free information, the consumer is still left with certain undying questions: What should "**I**" do and how should "**I**" go about doing it? The available literature usually directs the homeowner to seek the advice of a professional advisor to determine what's best for their particular situation. Who should that professional advisor be?

How To Get Compensated For Mortgage Planning

Now that we've determined that there are numerous factors to support the need for mortgage planning, the burning question is how do you get paid for providing it. Well currently financial services professionals (FSPs) are compensated in a variety of ways. They may receive a salary, initial and renewal commissions, service fees, client paid direct compensation, yield spread premiums, 12(b)(1) fees, investment management fees, brokerage commissions, expense reimbursements, and co-operative programs, among others. What's more is that there are FSPs who work for free with the hopes of being paid on the sale of various products or services that a client or potential client would need in the execution of the plan provided. This means that they are working on a 100% commission basis. There are also FSPs who work on a fee and commission basis. Additionally, there are FSPs who work on a fee-offset basis (they charge a fee but credit any commissions received against the fee).

Some of the same ways stated above of being compensated hold true for mortgage planning. Most commonly, currently "mortgage planning" is offered for free in hopes of being paid for a mortgage transaction. However, mortgage planning is also offered as a stand-alone personalized consumer service that is independent of the mortgage transaction or any other product or service just like fee-only financial planning that is provided completely separate and distinct from the sale or acquisition of any investment or investment advice, insurance, accounting, legal, or banking product. Although other forms of compensation maybe fair and reasonable, fee-only compensation will more likely avoid potential conflicts of interest or any appearance of impropriety. Offering mortgage planning on a stand-alone basis may also promote self-regulation and self-policing of this growing industry.

Just as homeowners have come to recognize that they must be vigilant by paying for a home inspection before a home purchase, they will realize that they have to be just as vigilant when it comes to the evolving mortgage market. Overtime mortgages cost the homeowner multiples of the home's purchase price (generally two and a half to eight times their annual income at the time of purchase) and mistakes in mortgage choices sometimes come with a very hefty price tag. So as more and more homeowners find themselves ensnared by a mortgage trap of their own making, fee-only mortgage planning services will become the norm as it becomes clearer that the free pamphlets and generalized free mortgage advice is not working.

Following a standardized format will allow you to provide mortgage planning for a basic flat fee in line with the cost of an appraisal or home inspection or you can establish an hourly fee schedule. How you set your fees is completely up to you. However, you should disclose your fee upfront and it should be stated in the mortgage planning engagement letter as discussed in Chapter 2.

Although compensation is important to any provider of service, in mortgage planning, just as with many other services, a possible sale or the amount of compensation to be paid by the client could shift the concern of the provider to their own outcome rather than the processes used in the provision of service or in producing an outcome that is beneficial to the client. While there is no doubt that compensation would rank high in the minds of those providing mortgage planning services, it must not overshadow the professional quality of the services rendered. Just like financial planning should be, mortgage planning should be about the process, the intelligent coordination of client goals and objectives, and benefits to the client.

No matter how the mortgage planner and client choose to structure compensation, mortgage planning can be more affordable to the average consumer than traditional comprehensive financial planning, and because mortgages are extremely common to a wide spectrum of consumers meeting various socio-economic demographics, mortgage planners can be more approachable and more easily accessible.

Summary

With the growing need for mortgage planning and the wide divergence of what practitioners mean when they speak of mortgage planning, in order to manage consumer expectations and start practitioners on the same page, there must be uniformity in defining mortgage planning and its underlying processes. In other words, mortgage planners should all speak the same language and use that language when communicating with the consuming public. Like the financial planning process, the mortgage planning process must be adhered to voluntarily for the betterment of all mortgage planners and the advancement of mortgage planning as a profession. (The mortgage planning process is described in detail in the coming chapters.) Additionally, mortgage planners must be mindful of the need to maintain high ethical standards. Although mortgage planning is not regulated on the state or federal level, in order for mortgage planners to safeguard the continued acceptance of mortgage planning by consumers, state and federal regulators, maintaining high ethical standards is critical.

The opportunity exists to catapult mortgage planning into a highly sort after worthwhile specialty satisfying not only the consumers' need for professional independent mortgage advice and a connection between mortgage decisions and their overall financial goals and objectives, but it's also an opportunity for mortgage practitioners to broaden the consumers' view of the mortgage services that can be offered beyond mortgage origination.

The precarious position of many homeowners as it relates to their mortgage demonstrates an obvious need for mortgage planning. Accordingly, those who now practice as mortgage planners and those who would like to be mortgage planning professionals should see the possibilities of making a valuable contribution to society and to protecting the financial strength of the American family through the practice and promotion of this financial specialty.

Chapter 2

Relationships That Lead To Mortgage Planning Opportunities – It Really Is Who You Know That Counts

"This is the true joy in life, the being used for a purpose recognized by yourself as a mighty one; the being thoroughly worn out before you are thrown out on the scrap heap; the being a force of nature instead of a feverish selfish little clod of ailments and grievances complaining that the world will not devote itself to making you happy."

- George Bernard Shaw -

Mortgage brokers by definition act as intermediaries who, for a fee, bring together borrowers and lenders to effect loan transactions. This status is recognized in state law. For example, in the state of Georgia, according to O.C.G.A. §7-1-1000(11) a "mortgage broker means any person who directly or indirectly solicits, processes, places, or negotiates mortgage loans for others, or offers to solicit, process, place, or negotiate mortgage loans for others or who closes mortgage loans which may be in the mortgage broker's own name with funds provided by others and which loans are assigned within 24 hours of the funding of the loans to the mortgage lenders providing the funding of such loans." Mortgage originators can and do create a relationship with a borrower where upon they (1) represent the borrower in the transaction, (2) represent the borrower, but receive a fee from the lender or (3) represent the lender. A mortgage originator can act as an agent for the borrower. In some states, the mortgage broker is a fiduciary to both the borrower and the lender.

The National Association of Mortgage Brokers (NAMB) claims that, "…two out of three Americans chose a mortgage broker to help them obtain a mortgage loan. Why? Mortgage brokers are experts in analyzing, structuring, underwriting, packaging and negotiating loan proposals. As independent real estate financing professionals, they have direct access to hundreds of financing sources to help you find a loan program that will be the best fit for your individual circumstances. And because mortgage brokers work with all types of credit and income parameters, they have been able to obtain financing for homebuyers who might otherwise have been unable to own their own home."[11]

Can mortgage brokers/originators do more than solicit, process, place or negotiate mortgage loans for others? Yes they can. Generally, there are no prohibitions against a mortgage brokerage business offering products and services, for a fee or commission, in addition to those offered in conjunction with the loan origination process. For example, Florida Statute 494 allows real estate, insurance and appraisal commissions so long as they are disclosed to the applicant. It's in that same light, fee-only mortgage planning should be provided. Being that there are no federal or state prohibitions or licensing requirements, what stands between you and the practice of mortgage planning? You.

Are You Ready To Be A Mortgage Planner?

If you are an outside mortgage originator/mortgage broker, you know that you don't get paid unless you produce results, that is until you make a prospective homeowner or existing homeowner happy or satisfied enough to close on "some" loan program. You don't get paid until the client says, "I do." This type of mortgage originator/loan officer operates much like an attorney who offers to represent a client on a contingency fee basis. In the case of a mortgage transaction, nothing comes out of the client's pocket upfront except the appraisal and maybe the credit report fee, and in the case of the attorney, maybe court filing fees.

Mortgage originators have an incentive to advertise or otherwise make known a variety of programs that address the concerns of prospective borrowers. A mortgage broker may represent many different lenders and unlike a lender they have no ongoing risk (they invested time and paper); thus after a loan closes, there is generally no recourse against the broker. Their goal, like many homeowners, was to get the borrower in. How long he stays in is up to the borrower.

If your focus has been primarily on the sale and on getting the client to funding at all costs, where does mortgage planning fit in for you? Can you look at a client and shift your thoughts from loan availability to loan suitability? Is a process that's centered on the client and on helping the client make mortgage decisions that are in line with his/her financial goals and objectives for you? You've got to know yourself well enough to answer these questions honestly. Your ability to be a good mortgage planner depends on it. It really is whom you know that counts, and the person you must know most of all is you.

What's Motivating You To Become A Mortgage Planner?

You don't have to be an economist or a marketing wizard to know that everything for sale isn't bought, that in addition to having a supply of something to sell, there has to be a demand for it. People may buy what they need and even more of what they want; and what they want most is to be made better off. We also know that "things" happen in spite of the profit motive, often for reasons that aren't always financially related.

Have you ever done something just to be nice or because you thought it was the right thing to do? Hopefully, the answer is yes. Altruism is a motivator. You sometimes do nice things for others because it makes you feel good, alive, or human. It's done voluntarily and with no monetary profit in mind. The personal benefit to you is usually an intangible benefit.

Gil Amelio and William L. Simon in their Book, *Profit From Experience,* say that a Vision is a statement of what a company wants to become and a Mission Statement is a more precise description of what a company does. They cite for example what guided Johnson & Johnson's immediate response in October 1982 to reports that seven people in Chicago where dead after taking Extra Strength Tylenol. It was reported that an unknown suspect(s) tampered with the product adding cyanide to the capsules after they had been placed on store shelves. Although Johnson & Johnson knew they were not responsible for the tampering, they immediately recalled approximately 31 million bottles of Tylenol nationally at a loss of more than $100 million dollars and halted all advertising of the product. The first line of the company's mission statement was given as the reason for the quick response. The first line of the company's Credo written more than 60 years ago, "We believe our first responsibility is to the doctors, nurses and patients, to mothers and fathers and all others who use our products and services."[12]

In the first edition of Richard J. Leider's book, *The Power Of Purpose,* published in 1985. Leider cites Peters and Waterman's book, *In Search of Excellence*, and emphasizes, "Top executives of excellent companies ensure that no corporate decision affecting internal or external practices goes against the company's purpose." Leider goes on to say that, "They understand that real commitment does not come through autocratic power, but through the power of purpose and caring. In such companies, leaders go far beyond 'what's expected' in business life to care for employees and to serve the larger communities surrounding the business. Every organization of value that shows successful growth and profit and makes significant contributions to its field needs the very kind of person it's least likely to accept. Every organization needs a few 'cutting edge' people who question where they are going, who challenge the old visions and offer new ones."

Recognizing that companies may be disturbed and insecure when a new vision is presented or their rules, methods and beliefs are questioned, Leider reminds us of the dictionary definition of "integrity". Leider provides both a dictionary definition and eventually one of his own, 'Integrity means living and working on purpose."

From a practical standpoint, Leider reminds you to think about the individuals you know who "live their values" and compare them to the one's that don't. Leider reminds you that when we interact with honest people you have a high level of trust that their promises and values will be lived. Less honest people make statements that are vague, unclear or confusing and although individuals and companies may intend to live up to their word, you must compare their words to their actions. Leider sums it up when he says:

> "*Purpose is a decision and a process. Purpose is something you live every day. It's not something to be delivered – it's to be acted upon. It's a process of directing and organizing your day-to-day life experience. Purpose means focusing on what deeply satisfies you, occupying yourself and your time with people, commitments, ideas, and challenges that help you feel worthwhile and make a difference. A purpose*

often comes in unexpected forms and packages. It surprises us."[13]

In determining your motivation for becoming a mortgage planner, one of the first questions you must ask yourself is why do you want to be a mortgage planner? After answering that question, dig deeper by asking these questions: What is your bottom line interest in being a mortgage planner? How will being a mortgage planner enhance or improve your career? What do you believe will be the biggest benefit to you in being a mortgage planner? After answering those questions, think over your answers and make a list of the reasons you want to be a mortgage planner. When you review the list, do you see a pattern of any kind? More than likely, two broad categories of motivations will become apparent, profit and service. Are your motivations more profit driven or service driven? Or are your motives a balanced combination of both? However your motives stack up, the crucial question is will your motives hamper your ability to act in the best interests of your clients?

So Today You're A Mortgage Planner. What Do You Do Today That You Didn't Do Yesterday?

How does your status as a mortgage planner change your outlook toward your clients? What do you do for your clients today that you didn't do yesterday?

Well it starts with a new way of viewing your business approach. Is your business approach client-centered? Is your business objective to provide the best products, best cost or best total solution that you can to your clients? If the answer is no, then that's what you start to do differently today than you did yesterday. Mortgage planning is about bringing professional unbiased guidance to consumers and homeowners and doing that puts the primary focus on the client.

To understand what you will do differently consider how you did business yesterday. The following questions are a checklist to help you evaluate your business format against what you really do and what you aim to do.

Question Checklist

- How do you currently advertise your availability to clients?
- What is the emphasis of your advertisements?
- Do you advertise that you have greater knowledge, expertise or skill than the ordinary practitioner?
- Do you claim to be, know or do something that you aren't, don't know or don't do?
- Do you create false expectations by promising things you can't guarantee or deliver?
- Do you alter or change your advertising emphasis depending on the medium used?

- Do you disclose your capacity/role and relationship with each and every customer/client in writing?
- What title do you use on your business cards?
- Do you disclose why you believe you are qualified to help?
- Do you serve in a fiduciary capacity or a sales capacity?
- Do you have a system for screening and qualifying clients?
- Do you adequately prepare for and give appropriate attention to the work that you do?
- Do you document the responsibilities you've undertaken?
- Do you document whom the client(s) is/are and their responsibilities?
- Do you document the compensation arrangements in writing?
- Do you document your willingness to work with a client's other advisors?
- Do you document your understanding of the complete and correct facts?
- Do you document decisions being made in a logical and methodical manner supported by facts?
- Do you document that all important areas of mortgage planning are reviewed?

- Do you in good faith and intent act in the best interest of the client based on all available facts?

Your answers to the above questions maybe an indication of something that you did yesterday that you will do differently today as a mortgage planner.

What Do You Bring To The Relationship?

Thinking back on the definitions of mortgage planner and mortgage planning, did that describe you and your way of doing business? If the answer is yes, congratulations! If the answer is no and you want to fit those definitions, what do you bring to the relationship as a mortgage planner that will get you where you want to be?

The definition of mortgage planning starts by stating that it is a client focused goal oriented process. This requires active listening skills, that is giving full attention to what others are saying and taking the time to understand the points being made, asking questions as appropriate and not interrupting at inappropriate times. It requires the ability to observe, receive and otherwise collect information from all relevant sources. Your actions should reflect what you've heard from the client. However, you are not an order taker. If the client had the answers, they wouldn't need you. Your professional skill is to take the verbal and written information from the client and to synthesize that information into a viable plan of action.

The next part of the definition of mortgage planning calls for the efficient allocation and management of a mortgagor's resources and risks. Careful consideration must be given to the best uses and scarcity of those resources and to potential increases in post mortgage expenses. This requires the ability to ask more probing questions. For example, the mortgage application captures the income, expenses, assets and liabilities as they existed before the mortgage and the purchase of the new home. However, it is very common that the purchase of a new home is followed by the purchase of other big-ticket items like furniture, appliances, and even cars. Additionally, if the mortgagor is purchasing a larger home, there will be increases in utility costs as well. None of these type expenditures and new payments are typically reflected in the debt-to-income ratio for mortgage qualification. You must go beyond the obvious mortgage application and underwriting type questions. That's one of the reasons they need you, to help them see their financial picture as it will soon be post new mortgage.

The definition of mortgage planning goes on to state that you should take into account the mortgagor's lifestyle goals and objectives with due consideration given to the mortgagor's personality and socioeconomic environment. As you are helping the consumer/homeowner plan, it will not help if you are making recommendations that change the people they are. If your recommendations don't fit together with who they are, the plan will be followed (or considered) for about as long as it takes you to present it. Therefore, you must have the ability to put your personal biases aside and see the clients for who they are. Someone who lives a rather flamboyant lifestyle isn't likely to follow a mortgage plan that shows them how he or she can afford the big fat mortgage in a country club neighborhood at the expense of other aspects of his or her lifestyle. Likewise, your skills as a mortgage planner may be questioned by a client that is adverse to debt if your plan recommends a bigger mortgage than the client feels comfortable with.

Your role is not to change your clients, but to guide them based on their individual characteristics. However, your recommendations must be truthful, objective and grounded by the client's prioritized goals. Part of the job of being a professional is being able to deliver news that is difficult to swallow, hard to accept or is just plain unpleasant. While the client may not want to hear it, it's your job to say it.

Lastly, the definition of mortgage planning states that you should arrive at the most appropriate mortgage decision under the circumstances. In helping your clients determine what's most appropriate, one of your biggest tools is maintaining objectivity and one of your best defenses is documenting that objectivity. Your goal is to deliver the most appropriate mortgage plan based on the client's stated goals and objectives given his or her resources, risk acceptance or aversions, lifestyle goals, personality and socioeconomic environment.

The quality of your mortgage planning is both a function of your knowledge, skills and abilities and the rapport you've developed with your client. All you know is what you know at the time, and you can't know what they won't tell you. Therefore, being a good mortgage planner depends in part on your clients feeling comfortable that what's said or provided in the mortgage planning engagement stays there. It's up to you to convey that sense of security and confidentiality.

By definition, a mortgage planner follows the mortgage planning process and recognizes the mortgage on a primary residence as part of a client's total portfolio. How do you recognize the mortgage on a primary residence as part of a client's total portfolio? It's really quite simple. Rather than ignoring this big fat liability, you help the mortgagor figure out how to manage it just like an advisor that might be hired to manage any investments in their portfolio.

A mortgage is not just a commodity to be obtained quickly and cheaply; because of the long-term financial consequences its treatment should be part of a consumer's financial plan. We have said that how the mortgage is managed impacts other aspects of a client's financial future. Rather than offering financial planning that works around this obligation (mortgage planning is not a traditionally recognized financial planning specialty like retirement planning, tax or investment planning), any defensible financial plan should acknowledge the existence of the mortgage and the need to help consumers establish a plan to manage, monitor and ultimately retire this debt as appropriate. For example, the benefits of structuring a mortgage repayment strategy or a reverse mortgage can be just as significant, if not more so, than speculative returns or even guaranteed returns on assets and investments, not only that, but the financial benefits of prepaying a mortgage or a payout from a reverse mortgage can be quantified and guaranteed with specificity.

For most financial planners, the mortgage is the elephant in the room. You see that it's there, but you don't really know what to do with it so you walk around it. So it is with financial planning where you typically walk around the mortgage and concern yourself with the discretionary funds that are left after the mortgage is paid. However, integrating mortgage planning into a comprehensive financial plan or investment strategy provides an anchor for all other aspects of the financial plan. In the future, it may be impossible to justify the suitability of other financial recommendations or to defend a financial plan that does not include adequate emphasis on mortgage management.

The definition of mortgage planner also calls for one to be capable and qualified to offer mortgage planning services up to the evaluation level (the highest level of Bloom's Taxonomy). Being able to evaluate your findings demonstrates the highest level of learning. In other words, you know what to do with what you've found. Consumers and mortgagors are looking for personalized mortgage answers and the ability to evaluate information and circumstances will result in the kind of answers they need.

The last part of the definition of mortgage planner states that high ethical standards must be maintained by not promoting fraudulent or unethical mortgage practices. The bottom line here is just doing the right thing. The American College Professional Pledge (the pledge is signed by all Chartered Life Underwriters (CLU)) says it best:

"In all my professional relationships, I pledge myself to the following rule of ethical conduct: I shall, in light of all conditions surrounding those I serve, which I shall make every conscientious effort to ascertain and understand, render that service which, in the same circumstances, I would apply to myself."

Cultivating Your Advisory Skills

In mortgage planning there is no product to sell. Your client is seeking your professional advice only. This is not the time to sell a mortgage or any other financial product. Blending planning with selling can interfere with your ability to provide unbiased advice. Understandably, moving from salesperson to planner may require cultivating or improving your skills as an advisor.

Your role as mortgage planner involves a high level of client contact. Therefore, strong interpersonal skills are the foundation of your success as a good advisor. Good listening skills and an understanding of basic human nature are also essential. You must have a genuine desire to understand your client and your client's situation. Mortgage planning is service oriented – you are looking for ways to help your client. Your ability to get the job done involves the following skill set.

- Strong Interpersonal Skills – Includes the ability to manage your emotions, behavior and motivations and to gauge and understand the same in others. You must be aware of your own strengths and limitations during face-to-face interactions. Patience is crucial. You must be able to develop empathy – the ability to put yourself in the other person's shoes, which is to see things from his or her point of view. You should be sensitive to the needs of others and to the forces that shape the way that others feel and behave. You will need to know how to convey information verbally and non-verbally. To succeed at a high level you need to have writing, speaking, presentation, communication and leadership skills among others.

- Active Listening Skills – This is a particular way of engaging in a conversation in which attention is focused primarily on one person, whereby you are fully engaged in absorbing and responding to what your client is saying. Eye contact is crucial to conveying that you are interested in what your client is saying. A friendly, relaxed and direct facial expression will convey that you are listening attentively.

  An active listener makes a variety of responses. You may encourage your client to continue or elaborate on what he or she is saying. You can do this by simply nodding your head, saying "Mm hm," or asking specific questions designed to encourage your client to go further into a response. Your expressions and responses should not be done in a perfunctory or inattentive way, otherwise it may appear as if you are not listening. Restating what you've heard is another way to respond that shows active listening. This way you are demonstrating that you have internalized what was said and understand it. Don't just repeat what you've heard, put it into your own words.

You can check your comprehension by saying something like, "If I understand you correctly, what you are saying is..." If you did not understand correctly, this gives your client a chance to clarify any points necessary. Being explicit about your understanding of your client's feelings not only allows you to make sure you are interpreting correctly, it also sends a message that you are empathizing with your client. You may also summarize what you have heard by restating the main points.

When practicing active listening, remember there are several things you should avoid. You should not interrupt your client or change the subject. Perfunctory responses should be avoided. You should also avoid changing the conversation by asking questions that lead in a different direction from what your client is saying.

- Problem Sensitivity – You must develop the ability to tell when something is wrong or is likely to go wrong. In short, you must develop the ability to recognize a problem. In being able to recognize problems you must be able to move beyond your self-imposed boundaries and deal with any limiting beliefs you may have.

- Inductive & Deductive Reasoning Ability – You must be able to combine pieces of information to form conclusions and have the ability to find a relationship between seemingly unrelated events. This involves identifying underlying reasons or facts and breaking down information or data.

- Critical Thinking – Requires the ability to apply logic and reasoning to identify strengths and weaknesses of alternative solutions or approaches to problems.

- Make Judgments and Decisions – You should have the ability to consider the relative costs and benefits of potential action steps and choose the most appropriate one. You should be able to explain complex issues in common language so that your clients without financial knowledge will understand your recommended plan of action.

Having a mortgage is a very common denominator for millions of people and there are many more everyday that hope to become mortgagors. Are you ready to bring what they need to the mortgage planning relationship?

Recognize The Uniqueness of Each Client

Now that you know you're ready for a relationship as a mortgage planner, you've got to prepare your client. In establishing and defining the client relationship, you and your client should start by discussing the client's objectives and expectations as it relates to the mortgage. You can explain to the client the benefits of mortgage planning, how you operate as a mortgage planner and how what you do and how you work sets you apart from others in your profession. However, you must recognize both your responsibilities and your limitations. You, as well as the client, must realize that historically, legally and financially they, the mortgagor, bears sole responsibility for all mortgage related decisions. You can guide and consult, but the ultimate decision always rests with the client. You never have discretion.

You should feel no apprehension during this initial step because you are not selling or pushing any product. There is neither a sales script you have to learn, nor are there any objections that you have to overcome. The question to ask your prospective client maybe as simple as: **Are you interested in exploring how effectively managing your mortgage can help you achieve your financial goals?**

In a one-on-one conversation, you should be able to explain that your mortgage planning services are for individuals who currently have (or who are contemplating) a mortgage and are interested in making some intelligent decisions regarding their money and their mortgage. A face-to-face interview should give the consumer a personal sense about you. Do you seem forthright in your answers? Do you provide a sense of trust and rapport? Are you focused on serving the client's needs, rather than focused on selling products?

Traditional financial planning resulted in planners screening clients by income, assets available for investment, specialized industry or occupational status such as self-employed professionals or corporate executives or by catering to middle and upper managers, etc. Mortgage planning provides a wide spectrum of potential clients, many of whom may have previously felt that they could not afford the services of a qualified financial planner.

Mortgage planning opens up the opportunity to find new clients no matter what the size of the mortgage or the level of the client's income. In fact, you should be better able to bring mortgage planning to a multitude of consumers that have never sought the services of any other financial planner. Incorporating mortgage planning into real estate, mortgage origination and other financial services professions will put mortgage-planning services within reach of the vast majority of Americans.

If you are offering mortgage planning as an enhancement to your existing practice, helping your clients manage and monitor their mortgage decisions in light of the ever-changing mortgage market should lead to improved client retention and to the growth of your client base. Even though the concept is very logical, in all likelihood, you will be the first to ever suggest (and are able to objectively explain and demonstrate) to your client how their mortgage decisions impact their ability to achieve other financial goals and how they can take a more active role in managing those decisions for their own benefit.

Mortgage planning presents an opportunity to increase the likelihood that prospects and clients see your professional value regardless of any products you may sell. Being that **mortgage planning can be offered before, during and/or after the mortgage transaction**, you will be able to serve a wide variety of potential clients.

Structuring the Mortgage Planning Relationship

When it comes to the structure of the mortgage planning relationship you establish with your client, there are several ways it can be structured. You may consider offering mortgage planning in a sales capacity as a stand-alone free service through your relationship with your client as a mortgage originator or real estate agent, or you may consider offering mortgage planning as a stand-alone service that is for a fee. It is best, however, to steer clear of offering mortgage planning with the intent of earning a commission on another service or product. Your desire to earn a commission may interfere with your ability to remain objective and in many cases a properly done plan or plan update may indicate that no commission or fee-paying product is needed. With a commission-based structure, your compensation method may clash with your ability to justify your recommendations and may keep you from putting your client's needs first.

If you choose to offer mortgage planning as a stand-alone free service in your sales capacity, mortgage planning will enhance the quality of service you already provide and may give you an advantage over others in your profession. With this structure, you should be upfront with your client and explain that mortgage planning is being offered as a courtesy free of charge, but that by providing the service you hope to build a relationship with the client that will lead to a future sale.

If you choose to offer mortgage planning as a stand-alone fee service, establishing a fiduciary relationship with your client can best accomplish this. A fiduciary relationship does not bar you from representing other interests (companies) during the course of other business dealings; however, during the provision of mortgage planning services, you would represent the client only. Being that mortgage planning is not regulated, there is no licensing required to offer this service on a stand-alone basis. You set the fee. You decide whether to set a flat fee or an hourly fee. And you set the parameters of the services you choose to provide. As a fee-only mortgage planner, with no conflicts of interest, you are not in competition with other financial service providers, for example, the client's investment advisor, mortgage broker, banker, insurance agent, attorney or real estate agent. There is no other financial service provider in your role. In fact, you should be able to coordinate your efforts with the client's other advisors to devise the best overall plan for the client.

Once you've made these determinations as to how the relationship is to be structured, it is recommended that an engagement letter be used to outline the services to be rendered, what's to be provided by the client and the amount of fees, if any, to be paid when the plan is complete. The letter should also state specifically how the fees paid by the client are to be determined, i.e., hourly or a flat fee. A **mortgage planning engagement letter** is a written letter that signifies the client's decision to move forward, which identifies the specific services that are to be provided, the capacity in which the planner services (salesperson, independent agent, trusted advisor or exclusive fiduciary representative), how the planner will be compensated, and the responsibilities of each party. Keep a copy of the engagement letter for your files and give a copy to your client.

Mortgage Planning Engagement Letter

- Who's responsible for what?
- What items will be covered in the plan?
- When is what due?
- How much will be paid and when is it due?

Summary

When it comes to relationships that lead to mortgage planning opportunities, start with understanding yourself and your motivations for becoming a mortgage planner. Assess what you can contribute to the relationship; determine whether your motives are profit driven, service driven or a combination of both. Your success as a mortgage planner begins here.

What you do as a mortgage planner may require a new view of your business approach. Mortgage planning should be client centered. Look to the definition of mortgage planning and mortgage planner in determining the need to change your business approach. Changes may also be required in order to cultivate your skills as an advisor. The skill set identified in this chapter helps you to stay client focused.

Each client is unique with his or her own objectives and expectations as it relates to a mortgage. Therefore, as a personal professional service, mortgage planning should result in answers that are tailor made to satisfy the concerns of each client. While the structure of the mortgage planning relationship is up to you, as a standalone fee-only service, there are no competing or conflicting interests. Whatever structure you decide to use should be captured in the mortgage planning engagement letter along with other aspects of the engagement that are best made clear from the outset to add clarity and to foster a good long-term relationship with your client.

Chapter 3

Data Gathering, Expectations & Reasonability – Where To Start

"Nothing has meaning in life except the meaning we give it."

- Anthony Robbins -

Now that you have established a mortgage planning relationship with your client what's next? How do you go about creating a mortgage plan? How do you live up to what you've promised your client? How do you show your client that you have professional skills beyond talking interest rate and fees?

Not only must you determine how to gather sufficient data (information) to develop a mortgage plan, but you've got to accomplish this through a process that manages the expectations of your client and that results in a reasonable (sound) and doable plan of action.

If you start by using a process that manages your client's expectations, the client should be very cooperative when it comes to gathering the information needed to develop the mortgage plan and when it comes to seeing the reasonableness and feasibility of the plan you provide. No need to panic. You've already passed this step. As you may recall, while you were establishing a relationship with your client you discussed your client's objectives and expectations as it relates to the mortgage; therefore, you've established the framework for managing the client's expectations of your mortgage planning services. It was that initial discussion that set the stage for what you've got to do next.

Gathering the Data That Forms the Plan

During mortgage origination, the focus is on numbers: income, length of employment, credit score, amount of assets, liabilities, etc. If the prospective client has a genuine interest in moving forward, there are certain documents and information you will need in order to adequately perform mortgage planning. The information you gather should help you gain an understanding of the client beyond the numbers.

- **ACTION STEPS**
- **INTENTIONS**
- **MOTIVATIONS**

You must also gather information that helps you understand what the client's overall financial goals (intentions) are, why they want to achieve those goals (motivations) and what they are willing to do to make it happen (action steps). If you are a mortgage originator, most of the financial data you need is collected on the mortgage application. However, in addition to that information, supplemental information must be gathered that helps you get to the financial objectives and motivations that underlie what's on the application and to financial information that's beyond the scope of a mortgage transaction.

In addition to using the information on the standard mortgage application, as a mortgage planner, you should also ask questions that will help you:

1) Refine or crystallize the client's goals
2) Develop an understanding of the client's values and attitudes
3) Recognize the difference between a client's objective (financial information) and subjective data (personal preferences and opinions)

As with most personalized services, being a good mortgage planner is a function of how well you listen to your client. Each client is unique. The advice and guidance you provide should be client specific rather than generalized "one size fits all" kinds of responses.

Ask the client to develop mission and strategy statements regarding their mortgage. In **Mortgage Based™ Financial Planning,** the **Mortgage Mission™ Statement** and **Mortgage Strategy and Investment Policy™ Statement** are a regular part of the mortgage planning service provided. The statements reflect a cognitive approach to mortgage decision-making. As will be explained below, these statements assist the Mortgage Based™ Financial Planner in preparing any analyses necessary to document the suitability of their recommendations.

The Mortgage Mission™ Statement sets out the purpose and financial objectives of the mortgage and the client's rationale for seeking a mortgage based on the client's core financial objective(s). Its focus is on answering and documenting the question of "why" the client chose to obtain a mortgage and why a particular loan program was chosen. "Why?" That's a huge question in establishing mortgage suitability. Before the client gets into seeking an understanding of the differences between loan products, "exotic" or traditional, they need to understand (1) why they are seeking a mortgage in the first place and (2) why they are seeking a particular type of mortgage.

Here the client can focus on the real need for the mortgage or equity line of credit and on considering viable alternatives. The Mortgage Mission™ Statement describes in rich detail what the client plans to achieve and when, as it relates to acquiring, maintaining and retiring their mortgage. The intent is to make the client more aware of the reasons behind his or her mortgage choices. The client's stated objectives provide structure, rationale, and motivation. In determining mortgage suitability, the client's Mortgage Mission™ Statement documents "why" the chosen mortgage is suitable.

While there is no set format for the wording, in order to avoid future misunderstandings or conflicts of interpretation, this statement is best written by the client in the client's own words, then signed and dated. There should be no attempt to influence the client's viewpoint. Because it captures the viewpoint of the mortgagor it is not expected to be technical in nature. This does not have to be a lengthy statement. However, it should be long enough to capture the essence of the client's awareness and state of mind as it relates to his or her present financial situation and other mortgage related issues.

In writing a Mortgage Mission™ Statement, the client should not only give consideration to the necessity of the mortgage, but also to the need or desire for the term chosen, and the particulars of the loan program. The client establishes his or her own time horizon, stating what they wish to accomplish as it relates to their mortgage and when. The client could also describe their present standard of living and the standard of living that would be comfortable once the mortgage has been satisfied. For those who will reach retirement age during the desired term of the loan, consideration should also be given to the client's ability to maintain the payments after retirement. In that regard, social security benefits may also be a factor.

Consideration should not only be given to whether or not the client will retire during the term of the loan, but also to when the loan itself may be retired due to prepayment, refinance or the sale of the home. The client may desire to retire the mortgage prior to their expected retirement in order to reduce the strain on post retirement income. For example, this maybe a good strategy for anyone who anticipates having uncertain or unstable retirement income, anyone who anticipates having insufficient retirement income, or anyone who wants more financial freedom at retirement.

Thought should also be given to anticipated changes in income due to known upcoming changes in employment for the client or spouse. These factors also impact the suitability of the mortgage; therefore, the client's plans in this regard should also be reflected in the mission statement.

Just as in Mortgage Based™ Financial Planning, writing a statement such as this allows your client to focus on their ultimate financial goal. If it's financial independence, then it should be as they have defined it. Creating a mission statement helps the client to recognize and appreciate the value of the store of wealth represented by their home and helps to deter them from making costly mistakes. Even if the client is not in the market for a mortgage right now, having them prepare a mission statement and a strategy statement is their declaration of where they want to go and what their expectations are as it relates to their mortgage.

The Mortgage Strategy and Investment Policy™ Statement as provided for in Mortgage Based™ Financial Planning, describes with specificity the tactics and methods to be employed to maximize the benefits of having a mortgage while simultaneously minimizing the total costs of having it. Its focus is on answering and documenting the question of "what" strategy and policy the client chooses to employ in obtaining, maintaining and retiring a mortgage, including an explanation of how it relates to the loan program sought or being maintained. In determining mortgage suitability, the client's Mortgage Strategy and Investment Policy™ Statement documents "what" the client chooses to do and how they choose to do it. This statement is also best written by the client in the client's own words.

The Mortgage Based™ Financial Planner helps their clients determine how often to examine and review the strategy, tactics and progress of the plan. Factors to be considered in writing this statement include: (1) Is the client's mortgage balance higher now than when the home was initially purchased? (2) What is the client's primary source of income? (3) Would it be to the client's advantage to commit to a shorter mortgage term using either a fixed, adjustable or hybrid mortgage product? (4) How much more would the client save with a term reduction even if there is no change in rate? (This does not necessitate the need for a new mortgage, but causes the client to think about and address the issue of total cost.) (5) What's the expected gap (difference) between the purchase price and final price the client expects to pay for the home? (6) What is the client's target debt-to-income ratio? (It is best to set it lower than the underwriting maximums.) Maximizing the debt-to-income ratio is counter-productive to this process. The client should also note known or anticipated new debts or anticipated reductions in household income.

For example, a client's mortgage strategy may include a footprint for the use of nontraditional loans, i.e., how it's intended to be used, what's next, when refinancing or prepayment is expected to take place and so on. With a mission and strategy statement, the client is prepared to shop for a loan program that fits his statements rather than the client trying to fit into a loan program. In other words, the loan program that fits the client is the one that best fits with the client's mission and strategy statements. Therefore, no matter how complex the structure of the loan program, the client is prepared for what lies ahead.

If your client currently has discretionary income or has plans to free up income and desires to put those funds toward mortgage prepayment, the investment policy portion of the statement would reflect that as well. A plan to prepay the mortgage is considered to be the formation of a defensive portfolio position, according to the Mortgage Portfolio™ Theory. (See Chapter 10)

The clients' mortgage strategy should anticipate rate adjustments, balloon payments, prepayments and early debt extinguishments due to the sale of the property or repayment of the debt. This statement is intended to keep the client in a proactive position rather than a reactive position such that the client has the greatest number of opportunities available. From a proactive position certain problems can be avoided if anticipated and planned for.

The client's ability to formulate this statement will likely depend in part on your preliminary assessment of the client's situation. It may be necessary to calculate the differences in the financial impacts of options under consideration, assuming or presuming an outcome could add up to significant dollar losses for your client due to estimation error.

The client should be encouraged to let the investment policy portion of this statement reflect the client's attempt to build a sound hierarchy of investing. A right triangle is often used to symbolize building a sound financial foundation from the bottom up. The concept appeared in Medical Economics, April 30, 1984. In the illustration, a pyramid was used to demonstrate the hierarchy of financial instruments used for creating financial security. Generally, the level of risk goes up as you ascend the triangle.

Creating a solid right triangle of investing helps the consumer decide what is important to them and how much risk they are willing to take to achieve the desired result. In creating a solid right triangle of investing, having adequate insurance is a good start. For example, life insurance provides the consumer the ability to almost instantly create with a stroke of a pen and a few pennies on the dollar an estate equal to or many times greater than the value of a home and mortgage combined.

Census data shows that the median household is composed of 2.3 people, therefore, it is logical that a plan should be developed that protects the family whether the consumer lives, dies or becomes disabled. Along with a foundation of insurance (life, health and disability income insurance), the consumer should consider the need to set aside an emergency fund large enough to satisfy a period of unemployment or other such emergency. This fund provides some financial protection in case of prolonged illness or joblessness and it also satisfies concerns regarding liquidity. It may be best to earmark these funds by setting up an interest-bearing separate account. The general concerns regarding risk associated with being a property owner are generally covered by a homeowner's insurance policy, which should be reviewed for adequacy.

As a mortgage planner, the risks that you are more concerned with are risks associated with (1) the mortgagor paying too much for the home by way of home financing and repayment choices, (2) the mortgagor's failure to recognize the true value of home equity, (3) the mortgagor not being cognizant of risks assumed, and (4) the mortgagor accepting misinformation and biased advice.

Example of a Right Triangle of Investments

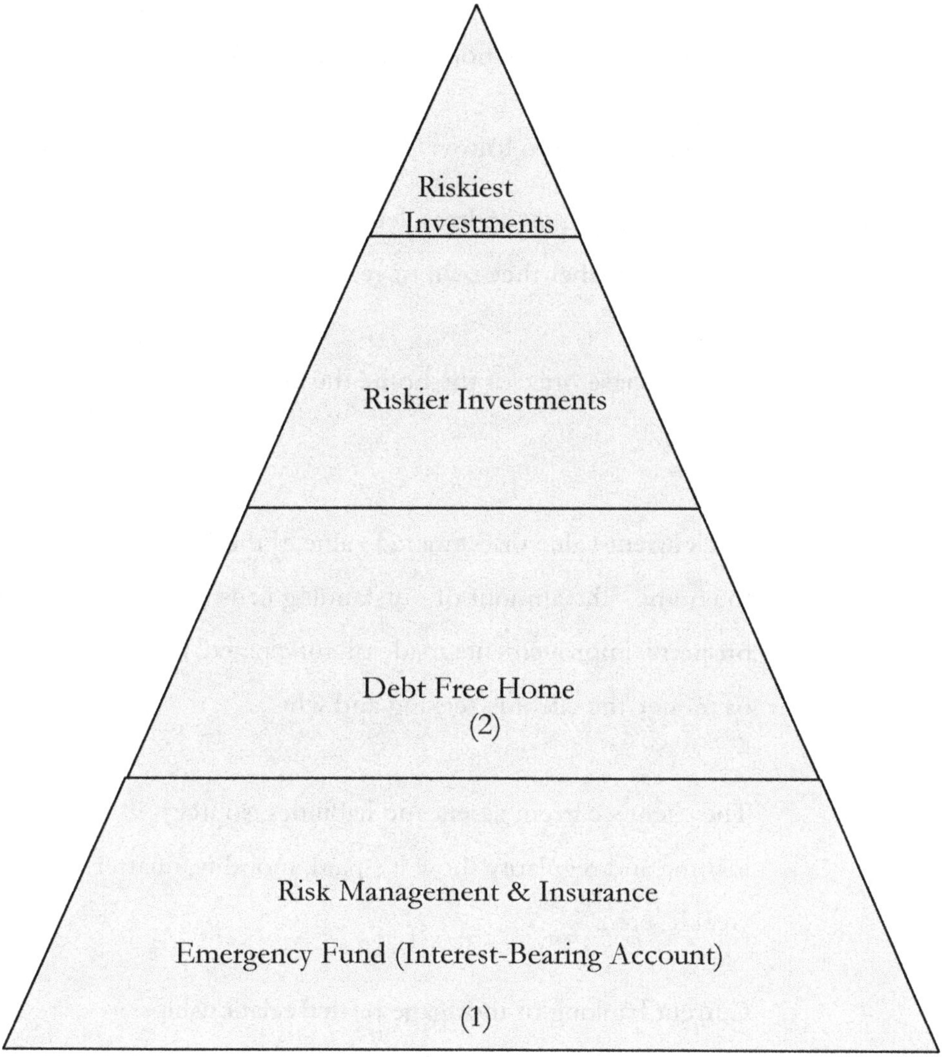

Along with being used to document the suitability and reasonability of your recommendations, the client written mission and strategy statements provide insight into the client's lifestyle goals, objectives and personality this will enable you to meet the definition of mortgage planning. You will also need to collect hard data by gathering documents such as past closing documents, tax returns for the past two years, financial statements, and insurance policies. You will need to know the following kinds of information about your client.

What you need to know:

Part 1. Name, age, current address, length of time at current address, whether they own or rent.

The purchase price of the home the client lives in or is seeking.

The current value or estimated value, if the client owns the home - the amount of outstanding liens on the property, improvements made or anticipated, the amount of money the client is seeking and why.

The client's current assets and liabilities, sources of income and regularity (how it's paid, monthly, quarterly, weekly, etc.).

Current banking or mortgage related relationships.

Ask meaningful questions to determine the client's acceptance and aversion of risk. (Also see Part 9.)

Determine the client's expectations with respect to the present and prospective property, for example the length of time the client plans to occupy the property.

Note what the client thinks about appreciation, cash flow, sales price, sales method, next planned move, and their mission, strategy, and any acceptable or relevant measure(s) of performance you or the client identify or may want to use.

Whether the client has funds for a down payment, if buying and the source of funds and/or how much equity the client wants to have or retain in the property currently.

The term over which the client wants to finance the purchase or refinance, the preferred loan product - fixed, adjustable or hybrid.

What is the client's current largest expenditure?

What are the client's plans for this expenditure? Does the client plan to eliminate the expenditure or sustain the expenditure and if so how, until when and why?

What variables can impact this mortgage plan either positively or negatively and how much influence does the client have or can they exert on the plan and the possible results?

Is the information the client has concerning their mortgage conflicting, confusing, or extrapolated from investment advice and misapplied to mortgages?

What are the client's second and third current largest expenditures? What are the client's plans for these expenditures?

What does the client expect to be their next major expenditure - home, car, college education, retirement, new business, etc.?

When does the client expect to use the money they are currently accumulating in their various investments? 1-6 months, 1-2 years, 2-5 years, 5-7 years, 7-10 years, 10-15 years, 15-20 years, or 20-30 years?

On what does the client expect to use the money they are currently accumulating in their investments - home, car, food, entertainment, clothes, education, business, etc.?

What is the source of the client's current income? What percentage of the client's current income is earned? What percentage is unearned or from passive sources? What are the actual dollar amounts for earned and unearned income and what are the client's expenses?

Does the client expect the amount of earned and unearned income to remain the same, increase, or decrease and over what time frame? 1-6 months, 1-2 years, 2-5 years, 5-7 years, 7-10 years, 10-15 years, 15-20 years, or 20-30 years? By what percentage: 1-5%, 5-10%, 10-15%, 15-20%, 20-30%, 30-40%, 50-60%, 70-80%, 90-100%, greater than 100%+?

Develop and/or ask other risk-return related questions as appropriate.

Part 2.

A summary description of the client's existing or proposed mortgage(s). The description should include rate, term, loan features, etc.

Part 3.

The overall costs of the client's existing or proposed mortgage including:

1) What the client needs to pay each month under the current terms of the loans - Interest only, interest and principal, and any mortgage

insurance. Assumptions about future adjustments, if any.

2) The total amount the client must pay back including the amount borrowed, a best and worst case scenario.

3) The stated or given interest rate.

4) The Annual Percentage Rate (APR) if a new loan is involved.

Part 4.

What the client needs to pay each month based on a specific loan amount and loan fees.

1) Interest or Interest & Principal Payment

2) Property insurance payment – not guaranteed–escrowed or not

3) Property tax payment – not guaranteed – escrowed or not

4) Mortgage Insurance Premium

5) Assumptions about the monthly payment if the payment is adjustable.

Part 5.

What are the client's mortgage costs relative to the current earned income? Mortgage as a percentage of earned income.

Part 6.

What are the client's mortgage costs relative to their unearned income? Mortgage as a percentage of unearned income.

Part 7.

What is the relationship of the client's mortgage to the value of the property?

What is the relationship of the client's mortgage to total financial assets?

What is the relationship of the client's mortgage to total non-financial assets?

What is the relationship of the client's mortgage to emergency reserves?

Part 8.

1) What is the relationship of the client's mortgage interest rate to current market rates?

2) Is the client's loan at, above or below current market rates based on loan amount, loan to value or term of their primary mortgage?

Part 9. What is the client's acceptance or aversion to mortgage risk exposures? For example, is the mortgagor paying too much for the home by way of home financing and repayment choices, is the mortgagor recognizing the true value of home equity, and is the mortgagor cognizant of the risks he or she is assuming?

1) How many months could the client pay their mortgage if their earned income suddenly dropped to zero?

2) How many months could the client pay their mortgage if their earned income suddenly dropped to zero due to their inability to work because of an accident or illness?

3) How many months could the client pay their mortgage if their interest rate increased 2% from their current rate(s)?

4) A 1% difference in rate based on the current balance represents $____ per month, a 2% difference translates to $ ______ per month.

5) How does the client feel about the terms of their existing or proposed mortgage? Is the client's interest rate risk matched to their interest rate tolerance?

6) Is the client's current interest rate a premium or discounted rate relative to their risk tolerance?

7) Is the client concerned about changes in short-term or long-term rates?

8) Is the client concerned with rate increases or decreases, why or why not?

9) If the client died prematurely do they own sufficient insurance to pay off their mortgage? Does the client need to or want to be able to do this? Can the client qualify?

10) If the client became disabled or sick do they have sufficient disability income or passive income to

pay their monthly mortgage? Do they need to or want to? If so, for how long?

11) Is the client maintaining or over improving the property?

Part 10.

Is the client unintentionally and unnecessarily liquidating and leveraging his or her property? Is the client unintentionally and unnecessarily assuming or retaining risk? Is there any undisclosed risk retention or assumption? Keep in mind, the higher the uncertainty the higher the risk.

Gather as much as you can of this information. Being that you're responsible for the content of your recommendations, taking time to ask the right questions will result in a reasonable well thought out plan of action such that you are able to help your client arrive at the most appropriate mortgage decision under the circumstances, given consideration to both how your client feels and the facts.

Data is collected for different purposes depending on your role. For example, the purpose of a mortgage originator collecting data differs from that of a financial planner and the client can and will disclose information to you as a mortgage planner that can't be asked by a loan officer or mortgage originator. As a mortgage planner, you can ask questions regarding anticipated increases in expenses or decreases in income. To further illustrate the point, as a mortgage planner you can discuss the client's plans to have three more children within the next seven years and the husband's plan to be a stay at home dad. These kinds of questions impact suitability and should be reflected in the client's mortgage plan. Also, the client can use you as a sounding board to discuss the financial implications of these type decisions.

Data collection is a critical step in mortgage planning because if you don't ask the right questions, you can't provide the right answers. As a mortgage planner, you get to ask questions others can't ask or don't know to ask. Your relationship with the client is different and the way you interact with the data is different. Therefore, your analysis and recommendations can be more complete, exact and accurate. Thus, the mortgage plan will better reflect the client's goals and plan of action to achieve those goals.

Summary

The data gathering process used should help you manage the expectations of your client and result in a reasonable and doable plan of action. Information gathered will help you understand what your client's intentions are, what his or her motivations are, what action steps will result in achieving the desired goal if followed, and what action steps will most likely be followed by your client. This is how you get to know your client. A well thought out plan is of little value if the action steps you've recommended are not in line with individual characteristics of the client. Attention to detain is critical. Be as specific as possible with your questions and insist that your client is just as specific with the answers.

Chapter 4

Benchmarks, Earmarks & Hallmarks – Marks That Mark The Plan –

"Principles are not practices. A practice is a specific activity or action. Practices are situationally specific, principles are deep, fundamental truths that have universal application. When these truths are internalized into habits, they empower people to create a wide variety of practices to deal with different situations. Principles are not values. Principles are the territory. Values are maps. When we value correct principles, we have truth. A knowledge of things as they are."

- Stephen Covey -
"The 7 Habits of Effective People"

The scientific method provides proof positive time and time again that in order to get the right answer you must at some point ask the right questions. Unfortunately, the problem(s) associated with asking the right question(s) is always complicated by how much we know or how much we think we already know, and how much or little we actually know.

This chapter functionally represents the intermediate step between collecting and gathering the client's information like that identified in Chapter 3 and analyzing and evaluating the data as presented in Chapter 5. As you will soon realize, benchmarks, earmarks and hallmarks differentiate a quality mortgage plan provided by a professional mortgage planner from all others. These elements help set the standards for professional mortgage planning.

What is the Mortgage Planner Benchmark?

What is the benchmark or standard of excellence by which mortgage planners can be judged? For example, whom can you ask for competent unbiased professional mortgage advice? Better yet who is qualified to provide such mortgage advice? How do you know they are qualified? What do they or others say that makes them qualified? Are they qualified because of their years of experience answering mortgage questions? How can you tell the difference between those with many years of experience answering questions with the wrong answers, from those who provided the right answers to the wrong questions, from those who provide the right answers to the right questions, from those who can give you the right questions to ask in order to get the answer you need? By what benchmark can we measure the Qualified Mortgage Planner™ (QMP) professional?

If no benchmark comes to mind, then it is up to the QMP™ professional to become the benchmark by which all other "mortgage planners" are judged. If the QMP™ professional is to become the benchmark, the question then becomes, what standard(s) exist that would enable you to feel comfortable accepting an answer from someone who claims to be a QMP™ professional? Would you be more inclined to rely on a legal standard, business standard, moral, ethical, religious, psychological, emotional or a scientific standard? Is there any one particular standard that encompasses most of the others?

Although one of the other standards may lead one to invoke a higher sense of obligation, in establishing a minimum standard by which a person or business can be held accountable as a QMP™ professional, lets explore a legal standard. With this standard, certain principles are called into play such as informed consent, full and fair disclosure, truth in advertising, fair business practices, ethics and evidence, and a reasonable duty to protect the public.

The Investment Advisors Act of 1940 ('40 Act) as amended in 1996, turned 66 years old in 2006. It's important to note as John Sestina did in *Fee-Only Financial Planning*, "the Investment Advisors Act of 1940 provided the regulatory framework for selling financial planning services on a fee basis."[14]

Since the '40 Act, as it is commonly called, was amended in 1996 and is appropriately credited and recognized for being the best available benchmark nationally for investment advisory services and serves as the model for most states securities statutes related to the regulation of investment advisers both registered and exempt from the registration requirements. What is interesting about the '40 Act is how its anti-fraud provisions are unlike (differ) the anti-fraud provisions in other federal security laws as it does not refer to conduct "in the offer or sale of securities" or "in connection with the purchase or sale of any security" in Section 206(1-2) or (4), it simply refers to conduct in the treatment of clients.

You can look at Section 206 of the '40 Act or its parallel citation in the United States Code, Title 15 - Commerce & Trade, Chapter 2D - Investment Companies & Advisers, Subchapter II – Investment Advisers, Section 80b-6 –Prohibited Transactions by Investment Advisers, more commonly cited as (15 U.S.C 80b-6). You'll notice that Section 206 of the Advisers Act (15 U.S.C 80b-6), states, "that it shall be unlawful for any investment adviser by use of the mails or any means or instrumentality of interstate commerce, directly or indirectly-- (1) to employ any device, scheme, or artifice to defraud any client or prospective client; (2) to engage in any transaction, practice, or course of business which operates as a fraud or deceit upon any client or prospective client" and 206(4), (15 U.S.C 80b-6(4)), "engage in any act, practice or course of business which is fraudulent, deceptive, or manipulative."

On its own website, the SEC states "Section 206 of the Advisers Act prohibits misstatements or misleading omissions of material facts and other fraudulent acts and practices in connection with the conduct of an investment advisory business. As a fiduciary, an investment adviser owes its clients undivided loyalty, and may not engage in activity that conflicts with a client's interest without the client's consent. In S.E.C. v. Capital Gains Research Bureau, Inc., 375 U.S. 180 (1963), the United

States Supreme Court held that, under Section 206, advisers have an affirmative obligation of utmost good faith and full and fair disclosure of all material facts to their clients, as well as a duty to avoid misleading them. Section 206 applies to all firms and persons meeting the Advisers Act's definition of investment adviser, whether registered with the Commission, a state securities authority, or not at all." Even though a QMP™ professional is not an investment adviser, depending on the facts and circumstances as they exist, the standard under the Investment Advisors Act of 1940 is an appropriate standard for any adviser, investment or otherwise.

While a QMP™ professional may or may not act in the capacity of a fiduciary, the Mortgagor Financial Representative™ professional (holder of the Residential Mortgage Planner® or Associate, Residential Mortgage Planner™ fiduciary mortgage advisor designations) does in fact maintain the highest standard of any mortgage planner, that of fiduciary. The mortgage planner should understand the difference between a fiduciary and an agent. A **fiduciary** is a "person having a duty, created by his undertaking, to act primarily for the benefit of another in matters connected with the undertaking." A fiduciary owes their client a duty of care and loyalty. According to Black's Law Dictionary, Seventh Edition, a fiduciary is *"one who owes to another the duties of good faith, trust, confidence, and candor."* Additionally, it defines fiduciary relationship as *"a relationship in which one person is under a duty to act for the benefit of the other on matters within the scope of the relationship."*

Black's Law Dictionary, Seventh Edition, defines **agency** as *"a fiduciary relationship created by express or implied contract or by law, in which one party (the agent) may act on behalf of another party (the principal) and bind that other person by words or actions."* It's also important to note that in a transaction conducted by an agent, the **principal** maybe partially (existence known but not identified), fully (notice), or undisclosed. It is also important to note that it is generally understood that an agent holds a position of trust.

The mortgage planner should be clear on whose behalf they are working. That is they should fully disclose their principal. The mortgage planner should also be able and willing to identify the principles that guide their actions and choices. The mortgage planner should understand the principles underlying the concept of a "conflict of interest". Recognizing that a **conflict of interest** is generally understood to mean a conflict between competing duties of a person in a position of trust, that is a conflict between a person's private interest and their public obligations.

Being that a mortgage planner may have had one or more different principal careers, here are a few of the principles of several other related occupations. Also note that the mortgage planner should be able to identify the legal relationship that exists between a client and various other real estate and financial professionals with whom a client or customer may work.

Real Estate Agents & Brokers - Generally, are considered fiduciaries to their clients and not a fiduciary to customers under most state laws. See NAR Code of Ethics. http://www.move2ut.com/Common/code_of_ethics.htm

Mortgage Brokers & Originators - May or may not be fiduciaries under state law. See NAMB Code Of Ethics. http://www.workingre.com/workingre/mb-codeofethics.htm

Investment Advisors - Generally considered a fiduciary under the law.

Registered Representatives - Not generally considered fiduciaries under the securities laws.

Insurance Agents & Brokers - Not generally considered fiduciaries under state insurance laws.

It is very important that a mortgage planner be able to distinguish between a "principal" under the law of agency and a principle that guides a person's conduct. **Principle** is commonly understood to mean a general or fundamental truth that may be used in deciding conduct or choice. The basic principles of "mortgage planning" come from the definition of mortgage planning.

The basic principles of mortgage planning are:

- (1) The primary focus is on the client,
- (2) Every client is unique,
- (3) Recognize the difference between efficient and inefficient resource allocation and management,
- (4) Recognize lifestyle goals and objectives given the client's preferences, priorities and resources, and
- (5) Help the client make the most appropriate mortgage decisions under the circumstances.

The Mortgage Planners Hallmark – The Mark of Good Quality

How do you make consumers aware of your allegiance to providing professional unbiased mortgage planning services? Adhering to a professional code of ethics and providing consumers a means by which to confirm your commitment to do this. A national registry free to consumers provides a means for Qualified Mortgage Planner™ professionals to increase consumer awareness of professional mortgage planning and of those dedicated to providing it.

The National Association of Independent Mortgage Service Providers (NAIMSP), a division of the Mortgage Institute For Financial Services Professionals, Inc. (MIFSP), provides one such registry for a nominal fee to listees. This national registry can be accessed by consumers free of charge and allows the consumer to confirm the existence of a Qualified Mortgage Planner™ professional (listee) by name. The NAIMSP Code of Ethics for Listees is also provided to consumers, which helps to set consumer expectations of the listee's chosen standards of performance.

Although the NAIMSP has established a registry for listees, including a listee code of ethics, membership in the association is for those who hold a designation from the Mortgage Institute For Financial Service Professionals, Inc. Members are authorized to act in the capacity of Mortgagor Financial Representative™ professionals and choose to practice in that capacity. The Mortgagor Financial Representative™ (MFR™) professional is a fiduciary that provides independent fee-only mortgage advice and who represents the mortgagor (the borrower) in making mortgage related financial decisions before, during and/or after the mortgage transaction. Members pledge to abide by the NAIMSP Code of Ethics for MFR™ professionals. The code of ethics for listees is not as comprehensive as that for members; however, the focus remains the same, providing good quality customer service.

NAIMSP Code of Ethics For Listees

Preamble:

Listees of the National Association of Independent Mortgage Service Providers are mindful that the soundness, usefulness, prosperity, and future of mortgage planning depend upon the honor and integrity of all persons engaged in providing mortgage planning service to the Mortgagor.

Listees shall conduct business in a manner reflecting honesty, honor, and integrity.

Listees shall diligently endeavor to be accurate in all advertisements and solicitations.

Listees shall not knowingly and deliberately make any misleading statements or promises to any consumer in an attempt to solicit business.

Listees shall not misrepresent or overstate their credentials, education, training, experience or professional status.

Listees shall endeavor to provide service and advice in the best interest of the client, to make fair and complete disclosure of all material facts, and to employ reasonable care to avoid client misunderstanding.

Listee shall provide to the client a letter of engagement signed by both parties at the onset of any fee services. The letter of engagement shall outline the services to be rendered and the fee to be paid by the client in order to avoid any client confusion.

Listees shall not deny equal professional services to any person for reasons of race, color, religion, sex, handicap, familial status or national origin.

Listees shall not discriminate, nor be party to any plan or agreement to discriminate, against any person or persons on the basis of race, color, religion, sex, handicap, familial status, or national origin.

Listees shall comply with all applicable state and federal laws and regulations.

Listees shall refrain from any conduct that would be adverse to the best interest and purpose of the mortgage planning profession. Members shall be forever vigilant of the importance of their role and shall conduct themselves only in the most ethical and professional manner at all times.

Listees shall endeavor to exemplify the highest possible ethical standards of all those who practice within the mortgage planning services industry.

There may be other registries available and other ways to hallmark your mortgage planning services. However, the NAIMSP Listee Registry offers a good and inexpensive way to mark the professional quality of the mortgage planning services you provide.

Earmarks – Knowing What To Do With Discretionary Funds

If your client could retire their mortgage, pay it off entirely, how much more money would be at their disposal? How much less money would they have to earn? How much less money would they need at retirement?

Frequently, consumers are advised to put their money in investments rather than prepaying their mortgage in hopes of getting a higher rate of return so that they can accumulate wealth. We recognize that it is easy to get swept away by the thought that money can be put out there somewhere to work such that it works harder than the individual has to. However, before taking risks without guarantees, your client should be prepared to handle those risks. The question is not should the consumer pay off their mortgage or put their money into stocks, 401(k) plans and other investment vehicles, but which one should be done first or how to establish a balanced approach that's in the best interest of the client. Being that the home is not considered to be a financial investment, mortgage planning and the mortgage plan are not intended for the provision of investment advice. However, it demonstrates the guarantees that come with structuring a solid mortgage action plan.

In Chapter 10 you will be introduced to the Mortgage Portfolio™ Theory, which is one of two theories that should be considered the underpinnings of mortgage planning (the other theory is the Mortgage Optimization™ Theory). It holds that a mortgage free home should be a defensive position in any portfolio and that prepaying the mortgage should be viewed just as favorably as any investment in the portfolio. **While investments are generally built around expectations of future performance; mortgage planning is based on guaranteed and/or contracted performance.** When funds are directed toward early extinguishments of mortgage debt, the outcome is guaranteed and the savings are quantifiable. Mortgage planning that includes a mortgage prepayment strategy can answer the questions that were posed above.

Most of us, including financial planners, are taught that if you have credit cards at 12 – 25% interest rate, you can get an immediate rate-of-return equal to at least the rate of your credit card simply by paying off the credit cards. There is no risk. It's a no-brainer. It has been common practice for financial counselors to recommend that consumers use the equity in their homes to pay off credit cards and other debts. However, most people are realizing that this advice has not lead consumers to a better financial position long-term. The typical consumer usually turns around and charges the credit cards up again. Additionally, by using the equity to pay off credit card debts consumers are putting their homes at risk for what was an unsecured debt. They are substituting an unsecured debt with a secured debt. In the event of financial hardship, most creditors are willing to compromise unsecured debts, which is better than putting a home at risk of foreclosure.

When the same question is asked in reference to the mortgage, the tendency is the same, to review the rates that have been historically available in the bond market (generally below the current mortgage market), then look to the only other market readily available to the average person and come to the realization, as history has shown, that stocks on average over the long-term out perform bonds and that small company stock out perform large company stocks, etc. Typically, historical market returns are used as proxies for future expected returns or performance even though past performance is no guarantee of future performance. Those <u>expected</u> rates-of-return are then compared to the interest rate on the mortgage, and then the same logic that was applied to credit cards is applied to mortgages.

Financial advice is often given as if the decision to prepay the mortgage or invest is purely a comparison of two investment options. Remember that the mortgage is a contractual obligation secured by the consumer's home. The consumer is asking you whether to put money at risk that could be used to satisfy a mandatory secured obligation that will swiftly lead to foreclosure if not satisfied.

In an article, entitled "The Pay-down or Prepayment of a Home Mortgage," John J. Spitzer, PhD and Sandeep Singh, PhD, CFA, *Journal of Financial Services Professionals,* November 2004, claimed that their study in considering the answer to the question of whether to prepay a home mortgage has "added to the common body of knowledge by deriving the conditions under which a mortgage should be paid off early compared with investing in a competing investment[15] of equal risk. Their study attempts to explain when consumers should prepay." These professors conclude: "current advice on the choice to prepay a mortgage or invest the money in a competing investment is flawed due to the failure to consider risk of the competing alternatives and the differential effects of taxes..." They recognized that an equity investment (for example, an individual stock or stock mutual funds) is never a suitable alternative to prepaying a mortgage because the risks are not equivalent.

Some would argue that equity in a consumer's home is the same as cash. It's just sitting there, and if it's not pulled out or liquefied, it's not at work. It's a wasted asset. However, it is quite the contrary. The money, as confirmed by the Mortgage Portfolio™ Theory, is working to reduce the amount of other money (capital) that must be at work, it's working to provide a tax-free way to save, it's working to reduce the amount of income that must be earned, it's working to reduce the amount of money (income) needed at retirement, and it is working to protect he home from risks associated with negative changes to the consumer's overall financial situation.

Be cognizant that comparing investing to prepaying a mortgage is an imbalanced comparison such that it does not end with disastrous results. Attention should be given to the risk to the home of pursuing a so-called "higher rate of return." Paying off the mortgage is a risk-free endeavor that reduces the borrower's liability with certainty. Comparing a risk-free payment to expected equity returns disregards the risk differential of the two options. Given this risk differential, it would be imprudent to dispense investment advice based solely on this type comparison. **No one has yet been able to identify an investment with comparable risk that provides the same level of benefit at the same cost as prepaying the mortgage.**

When it comes to investing, most responsible parties suggest that you first make certain the basic necessities are taken care of such as food, shelter, clothing and transportation. The next step usually involves the establishment of an emergency reserve and protection against the losses that could result from the loss of life, health, disability or liability (negligence). The decision then is what to do with what's left over or surplus. These are the funds available for investments or prepayments. The most natural and logical questions when investing are: (1) when will the funds be needed or wanted, (2) how much money is currently available, (3) how much will be needed and how long will it be needed, (4) where can the money be invested, (5) are there minimum investment limits, (6) how can the return be maximized for the least amount of risk, and (7) if there is a "higher risk tolerance", what kind of returns can be expected? Don't guess at the answers.

Financial planners typically provide advice on investments and consumer debt management. However, generally financial planners have been better trained to give investment advice than to give advice on mortgages. The reason for this maybe (1) the slant of most training for financial planners is toward providing investment advice or (2) planners and FSPs are most often employed by or earn their incomes through companies that distribute investments or financial products.

For a commission only planner, the monies not applied toward the mortgage(s) may be viewed as monies available for making commissionable investments. A mortgage creates a gray area for the average financial planner because it's the largest consumer debt and yet it's tied to what may be or generally is the client's biggest physical asset (their home). In this instance, advice should not be given on the debt without considering the impact on the asset.

If you want to provide your clients an objective mathematical method to quantify the answer of whether to prepay the mortgage entirely or invest, it can be found in the Mortgage Pre-payment Equivalent Yield™ (MPEY™), a calculation tied to the Mortgage Portfolio™ Theory. The MPEY™ is unique to each client and it's based on comparing the client's financial situation with and without a mortgage to investment options, and determining which direction the benefits flow by comparing any loss or gain in tax benefits, any loss or gain in real cash flow, and recognizing the tax free rental value of the property. The MPEY™ is a value that can be used as a comparison to the projected rate of return of any investment.

The focus of the MPEY™ is not just on the tax treatment of the mortgage or even the "alternative investment", but also on recognizing the trichotomy a mortgaged home represents as an investment, a physical asset, and a financial liability. The MPEY™ recognizes all three sides.

Summary

This chapter covered the benchmarks, hallmarks and earmarks that set the standards for differentiating between quality mortgage planning provided by a Qualified Mortgage Planner™ professional and all others. These marks identify the QMP™ professional's commitment to a customer-oriented approach to mortgage planning.

The QMP™ professional is the de facto standard and the benchmark by which all other mortgage planners should be judged. QMP™ professionals hold themselves accountable to standards that include principles of informed client consent, full and fair disclosure, truth in advertising, ethics and fairness in business practices, and a reasonable duty to the public. By becoming a listee in a national verification registry and agreeing to adhere to a code of ethics, QMP™ professionals can establish a hallmark by which they can be readily identified.

Additionally, identifying funds earmarked as discretionary funds is another intermediary step between data gathering and data analysis and evaluation. It's part of asking the right questions in order to provide the right answers. In accordance with the Mortgage Portfolio™ Theory, recognizing that prepaying the mortgage should be viewed just as favorably as any investment in the portfolio, QMP™ professionals should acknowledge that they could make a valuable contribution to the client's portfolio decisions without dispensing any investment advice.

Chapter 5

Data Analysis & Evaluation - What To Do With What You've Got -

"There's no better way to build a sizable client base, create recurring revenue streams, and promote and maintain client trust and loyalty than to serve the best interests of your clients. Whether the homeowner is looking for a mortgage, a second opinion on a mortgage, a Mortgagor Financial Representative™, or assistance in evaluating and retiring an existing mortgage, as a mortgage practitioner you want to be the only person the homeowner looks to before, during and after mortgage origination. These services help mortgage professionals be that person."

- Leon Morris -

For the average consumer, the mortgage acquisition process and the financial planning process can be reengineered through professional mortgage planning. Who would doubt that the efficiency of financial planning can be greatly improved with a consistent starting point, the recognition of the single largest debt most mortgagors have that's tied financially and emotionally to the single largest physical asset most people have? However, generally speaking, financial planning works around the mortgage and prides itself on being a middle-class need, while mortgage planning begins and ends with the mortgage and prides itself on filling the needs of all classes of consumers.

As a professional mortgage planner, you are responsible for your recommendations. Therefore, it is up to you to make sure that you start the data analysis and evaluation process with sufficient information to support those recommendations. If at the start of your analysis you determine that certain portions of the information gathered seems vague or that there appear to be gaps and inconsistencies, follow-up with your client, insist on specifics rather than generalities, determine if there are any extenuating circumstances that explain the inconsistencies, and ask additional questions to further clarify your understanding. If you fall short at all during the mortgage planning process, it's best to do it here where it can be easily corrected. If anything, your client will appreciate your thoroughness and attention to detail.

Using all information collected, including the client's mission statement and strategy statement, the QMP™ professional is ready to determine mortgage suitability by identifying problems and opportunities across major planning areas such as the client's asset and liability structure, cash flow, basic investment portfolio structure, and the general tax implications of carrying a mortgage. The documentation of your analysis should be sufficient enough that any other mortgage planner can pick up where you left off, if necessary.

There are two forms of analysis that the QMP™ professional can perform using the data gathered to help the client assess the suitability of his or her mortgage choices: Mortgage Fundamental Analysis™ and Mortgage Technical Analysis™.

Mortgage Fundamental Analysis™

The focal point of traditional mortgage analysis is the acquisition of a new mortgage (to fund a purchase, refinance or to add a second mortgage or line of credit). It is said that traditional underwriting is concerned with the four C's: credit, collateral, character, and capacity. So while traditional mortgage underwriting is concerned with the four C's, Mortgage Fundamental™ Analysis (MFA) is concerned with the individual consumer's financial position and goals and the appropriate matching of the two. The emphasis is on suitability. MFA involves assessing the answers to questions that traditional mortgage analysis does not ask or answer. Traditional mortgage analysis is focused on qualifying the consumer for a mortgage, a much lower threshold or form of suitability.

In Mortgage Fundamental™ Analysis, the answer to the traditional fundamental mortgage questions are also assessed and yet due regard is given to the personal financial goals and objectives, and financial likes and dislikes of the client while recognizing both the client's/mortgagor's personal circumstances and the role of the mortgage in their overall portfolio of holdings. In short, the financial facts (**objective facts**) of their situation are recorded and just as importantly, the individual **subjective facts (**how they feel, their expectations, their hopes and desires) as they have identified in the mission statement and strategy statement.

Beyond the expectation that the client will live in the property as a primary residence if so stated on the application, traditional underwriting can't ask the client, for example, how long do they actually plan or anticipate living in/occupying the property? The underwriter must look at the transaction based on its underwriting merits. The fact is the client and possibly the client's advisor know more about the pending transaction than the mortgage underwriter can ask. This is not to suggest fraud or manipulation of any kind. In fact, the implications are quite the opposite. The fact is, in order to properly serve the client's best interest, you, as the QMP™ professional, literally have to go beyond the traditional questions and disclosures and/or analyze the answers to those questions differently.

Questioning the client about how they feel about certain financial considerations is the qualitative approach to analyzing the client's particular situation, and as you ask questions (on the fact finder), you should listen closely and take good notes. As the client answers the critical qualitative questions, it's a good idea to restate their answer to make sure that you understand the client's perspective. You must also realize that some decisions are made for personal or emotional reasons regardless of the economic rationale, and although they may not be sound from an economic or financial standpoint, it just might give the client greater piece of mind, and sometimes you can't beat the perception or feeling that the client/mortgagor will be able to sleep well at night.

Being that MFA is a qualitative and quantitative analysis, once you have completed the analysis you should have a complete picture of the client's individual needs and desires, which helps you to become more sensitive to those needs and desires. Documenting your evaluation of not only what the client needs, but also what he or she desires supports your determination of suitability.

PROFESSIONAL MORTGAGE PLANNING ANALYSIS

MORTGAGE FUNDAMENTAL™ ANALYSIS (MFA)

Concerns the individual's financial position, goals and objectives, taking into account an individual's fundamentals.

MORTGAGE TECHNICAL™ ANALYSIS (MTA)

Concerned with the current supply and demand for the type of mortgage the client has, needs or wants, taking into account the individual's fundamentals.

Critical to this technical analysis is the source, amounts, and types of income a client receives along with certain specific property characteristics.

Mortgage Technical™ Analysis

Mortgage Technical™ Analysis (MTA) is an objective quantitative analysis that requires processing the numerical data gathered. MTA adds another "C" to the four Cs. The fifth "C" is cost. That is the price and availability of a mortgage and housing meeting the mortgagor's requirements and with helping the mortgagor identify and correct financial inefficiencies.

MTA takes into account the client's fundamentals and matches that with the current supply and demand for the type of mortgage the client has, needs or wants. If a mortgage currently exists, after it's determined that a mortgage is still necessary, the QMP™ professional determines whether or not the existing mortgage is currently at market, below market or at a premium rate for the term of the loan? To do this you must be able to evaluate price and costs. In doing so, consider the following:

- Your observations, findings and recommendations with regard to the relationship of the client's mortgage interest rate to current market rates. (Is the loan is at, above or below current market rates?)

- Your findings as to whether or not the client's current mortgage structure is serving the client's interests, given their goals and objectives (needs & desires) above and beyond the stated interest rate on the loan? Or is there a proposed structure that would better serve their needs?

In order to make a proper evaluation of the client's situation in Mortgage Based™ Financial Planning, the following MTAs may also be performed: Mortgage Ratio™ Analysis, Mortgage Risk™ Analysis, Mortgage Tax™ Analysis and a Mortgage Pre-payment Equivalent Yield™ (MPEY) analysis. Each of these will be touched on briefly below.

Mortgage Ratio™ Analysis

Mortgage Ratio™ Analysis is not performed to maximize the sale, but to maximize the benefits of having a mortgage during the time it's needed and to minimize the costs during the time it's in place. In other words, the goals of performing the Mortgage Ratio™ Analysis are to minimize the costs of the mortgage, minimize taxes paid by the client, minimize the risk of paying too much money for the residence over time, and to maximize the utility of the mortgage, such that the homeowner can realize the maximum benefits of true homeownership. The following ratios should be considered:

- Ratio of client's mortgage costs to the current earned income. Mortgage as a percentage of earned income.
- Ratio of mortgage costs to unearned income. Mortgage as a percentage of unearned income.
- Ratio of mortgage balance to the value of the property.

- Ratio of mortgage balance to total financial assets.
- Ratio of mortgage balance to total non-financial assets.
- Ratio of mortgage balance to emergency reserves.

By analyzing and providing the client the primary housing ratios, it helps the client focus their attention to the risk they take relative to their income, their discretionary income in particular, and a cost benefit analysis will show them where their discretionary dollars are going relative to what it is they are trying to achieve. The ratios also show, in simple terms, the primary source of their income so that they can better understand and recognize the interrelationship between income, the source of their income and the relationship it has to both taxes and the amount of risk to which they expose themselves. This understanding will guide them in determining when a particular strategy or course of action is or isn't suitable or appropriate in light of all known facts and circumstances.

The two traditional mortgage-qualifying ratios are:

1) The monthly housing expense (MHE) to income ratio (front end ratio), and
2) Total obligations to Income Ratio (back end ratio).

In the mortgage origination process, the purpose of loan to value analysis, from the borrower's perspective, has been to determine the total amount of cash needed at closing on a purchase transaction and in determining how much cash would be available in a refinance cash-out transaction or if they are subject to any PMI requirements on a rate term transaction, or otherwise meet loan program guidelines. The purpose of this analysis, from a mortgage planning standpoint, is to provide a check and balance on mortgage suitability and appropriateness given the alternatives and resources available to the borrower so that judgments can be made about particular financial or non-financial assets.

The objective of the purchase price comparison is to determine if the client is getting closer to full homeownership (a mortgage free residence) or further away and at what costs. The goal of ratio analysis is to provide a unit of measure and a benchmark for comparison purposes such that the ability exists to compare one month or quarter to another with the principal (overall) goal and/or the target goal for a particular period. If the client stays on target, this number should be increasing while other ratios are decreasing over time. For example (all else being equal, with an amortizing loan), the client who has a goal of homeownership should find that their MHE to earned income, unearned income or taxable income, and their loan to value, loan to purchase price, loan to total monthly obligations, and loan to rental value would be going down, while the principal to interest ratio would be consistently increasing.

When you analyze the ratio of the mortgage balance to what the client defines as emergency and/or available reserves, the objective is to evaluate the client's ability over time to make payments in the event the primary income source is interrupted or is discontinued for any reason.

This should be a number the client is comfortable with, for example 3-6 months of expenses as a reserve maybe considered reasonable, more or less maybe required depending on the particular circumstances of the client and could include such factors as the length of time the client thinks it would take to get another comparable paying job given the particular industry or occupation, or if relocation was necessary, the average number of days homes in the area are on the market for sale, along with relocation costs, among other things.

In doing that, Mortgage Ratio™ Analysis will help you determine how much the client has available that can be reasonably applied to the purchase price of the home and how much can be applied toward the mortgage over a particular period of time (month, quarter, several quarters or a year) and still leave an emergency cushion. Of course, the more funds applied toward the principal, the lower the overall costs of the mortgage (since interest is only charged on the outstanding balance and interest is charged based on time outstanding). Ratio analysis is also beneficial in pinpointing problem areas and in exploring the answers to other questions that will help the client move toward achieving their goals.

Mortgage Risk™ Analysis

Mortgage Risk™ Analysis is another valuable tool when it comes to determining mortgage suitability. It is performed to enable the client to make intelligent risk related mortgage decisions. Mortgagors take financial risks relative to having a mortgage on their property without being aware of the risk they are taking. Mortgagors take risks that are the result of cultural bias, attitude and/or financial myth. Mortgage risks should be consider when determining the amount of home and mortgage the client can reasonably afford. In performing this analysis, the QMP™ professional should ask questions that will help to distinguish between a client's willingness to assume risk and their ability to sustain or recover from a loss if the risk is realized.

One of the fundamental problems with risk is that homeowners may not fully recognize the risks associated generally with a mortgaged home and particularly with the loan product(s) chosen. The risk that's most familiar to the borrower involves the traditional obstacles to an approved application. After completing the Residential Mortgage Loan Application, the borrower is at risk of receiving an adverse action letter detailing why the application was declined, terminated or cannot be approved as applied for. For most borrowers the risk of an adverse action letter is of more concern than any other mortgage related risk. Therefore, in their zest for loan approval, they often open themselves to risks that may have long-term financially devastating impacts.

For a first time homebuyer, one of the risks that could be considered from the outset is the risk of making an improper rent versus buy comparison. With a QMP™ professional, the homebuyer can explore cost concerns that they may not want to discuss with their loan officer. These financial concerns may extend beyond those addressed in underwriting the loan. There are cost differentials, other than an improper calculation of the mortgage interest deduction, that impact the affordability of the home including the added expenses of home maintenance, increased utility costs, new household purchases (furniture, appliances, etc.), and homeowner's association fees. These kinds of cost considerations extend beyond the affordability of the mortgage payment.

There is also the risk of not shopping for the mortgage properly or early enough in the process. This risk applies to the first time homebuyer as well as the veteran borrower and includes risks associated with not knowing how the status of credit, employment, residency, collateral, and citizenship, among other factors (particularly those related to the actual pricing of products and options), can influence the mortgage shopping outcomes. Therefore, the borrower may not be aware of how to mortgage shop for their special needs, which can result in incurring avoidable costs. Here again is where the personal guidance of a QMP™ professional can result in significant cost savings for the borrower.

Of all the documents that are signed at closing, the two that are most relevant to Mortgage Risk™ Analysis are the promissory note and the mortgage (security deed, deed of trust, etc.). The document names may vary by jurisdiction, but regardless of name it is the mortgage documents that create the security interest in the real estate that secures the loan. While the security deed is recorded, the note may or may not be recorded; recording perfects the mortgagee's lien position. The mortgage allows the lender to foreclose on the real property securing the promissory note if the borrower is not repaying the note as agreed. Most lenders use a common form for the mortgage instrument to assure that it can be assigned to another lender or a member of the secondary mortgage market like Fannie Mae or Freddie Mac.

From the borrower's perspective, they may view the risk of foreclosure as the primary risk associated with a mortgage. From the mortgagee's perspective this is default risk, the risk that the lender will not receive interest and principal when due. Hence, while default risk is generally not a concern for the borrower, it is reasonable for the borrower to be readily aware of the foreclosure risk that leads to the loss of their interest in the property (title) if loan interest and principal are not paid as agreed. The following are some very real common reasons for failure to pay as agreed and certain steps that can be taken to mitigate the risk.

Loss of income – due to a loss of a job/employment - Establish adequate reserves and emergency funds equal to the period of time you think it would take you to find another job/employer; increase passive income, get a second job, build up other income or assets or reduce expenses.

Loss of Life – due to untimely death - Determine if eligible and acquire the appropriate amount of life insurance to replace lost earnings or pay off the mortgage due to an untimely death.

Loss of health – due to an accident or sickness - Determine if eligible and if appropriate, acquire sufficient disability income insurance, review Social Security disability eligibility and benefits.

Loss of Spouse – due to divorce (also see loss of income) or untimely death (also see loss of life).

Change in The Payment Amount – due to a change in the interest rate on a home equity line, adjustable rate loan, or a balloon payment being due. Maintain an easily accessible record of anticipated rate changes and planned/anticipated and responsive action steps that may for example include refinancing or paying off the mortgage.

These risks can also be mitigated with a paid for home. How much less concern would there be about any possible loss of income if the home were paid for? Would the homeowner be more self-insured or less self-insured, particularly if there is concern about qualifying for private life or disability insurance? Although there is some controversy among financial advisors regarding the benefits of prepaying the mortgage, how can one dispute that there are psychological and financial benefits associated with being debt free, not to mention that being debt free frees up capital for additional savings and/or investments without putting the roof over your client's head at risk.

While there are many reasons given for owning a home, state law and most loan documents covering residential mortgage loans do not consider the primary residence an investment. Hence, another real risk is the tendency to think of a home as an investment. This is not to suggest that a home doesn't have investment like qualities. However, as is discussed throughout this book, whenever paying off the mortgage is compared to investing those funds, it's an unbalanced comparison because the mortgage is a debt not an investment. Even though perspectives differ on whether or not a mortgage should be prepaid, by definition repayment of a debt involves ZERO investment risk.

The risks that aren't calculated or expressed mathematically in connection with the home relate to all the reasons the borrower bought the home in the first place and the reason why they currently occupy the home. The risk that at times may be difficult to value, hard to assess, is often implied, but seldom discussed is a lifestyle risk. Does the mortgagor wish to risk their chosen lifestyle failing to pay interest and principal when due?

Here are some questions that may be helpful in accessing mortgage risk:

a) Is the client concerned about changes in short-term or long-term mortgage rates?

b) A 1% difference in rate based on the current mortgage balance represents $____ per month, a 2% difference translates to $______ per month.

c) For how many months could the client pay their mortgage if their interest rate increased 2% from the current rate(s)?

d) How many months could the client pay their mortgage if their earned income suddenly dropped to zero due to job loss?

e) How many months could the client pay their mortgage if their earned income suddenly dropped to zero due to their inability to work because of an accident or illness?

f) How many months could the client pay their mortgage if their investment earned a zero rate of return or lost value; and how much loss (in dollars) of value is the client/mortgagor willing to accept before liquidating the investment?

The type of questions above will help you to assess the client's mortgage risk tolerances and to gauge the client's resilience to unexpected income changes.

Mortgage Tax Benefit™ Analysis

MTA may also include a Mortgage Tax Benefit™ Analysis. However, this service does not include tax return preparation, filing or amendment of a personal income, gift or estate tax return. Your client should look to his or her own tax accountant for these services. In conducting this analysis, the student should be aware of two relevant IRS publications, Mortgage Interest Deduction #936 and First Time Homebuyers #530.

As a QMP™ professional, it would be good to be familiar with how to (1) describe the mortgage interest deduction as it relates to the home acquisition and home mortgage equity limits and the effect of using mortgage proceeds to buy a business or investment and where the proceeds were used to improve the home; (2) describe under what conditions a wraparound mortgage interest is or isn't deductible; (3) identify the necessary components to accurately calculate the mortgage interest deduction for an individual, a couple filing a joint return, married filing separately, or head of household; (4) explain the significance of miscalculating the benefits of the mortgage interest deduction and, given the appropriate data, calculate the actual tax benefit of the mortgage interest deduction; (5) articulate under what conditions the mortgage interest deduction is or isn't a valid consideration in decisions to purchase or mortgage a home; (6) write the formula that would result in a proper calculation of the tax savings from mortgage interest; and (7) explain why the source of funds used to pay the mortgage interest is important.

As basic as it is, before performing the Mortgage Tax Benefit™ Analysis the first question a homeowner has to answer is do they have an existing mortgage? If they have a mortgage, is it secured debt on a qualified home? In making that determination, consider the definition of each of these terms.

Secured debt – A secured debt is one in which you sign an instrument (such as a mortgage, deed of trust, or land contract) that makes your ownership in a qualified home security for payment of the debt, providing that in the event of default the residence could satisfy the debt, and the instrument is recorded or otherwise perfected under any applicable state or local law.

Qualified home – This means your main home or your second home. A home includes a house, condominium, cooperative, mobile home, house trailer, boat, or similar property that has sleeping, cooking, and toilet facilities. The interest you pay on a mortgage on a home other than your main or second home may be deductible if the proceeds of the loan were used for business, investment, or other deductible purposes. Otherwise, it is considered personal interest and is not deductible. (Homes under construction, second homes rented out, mixed use properties, homes partially rented out, time-sharing arrangements, offices in the home, cooperative apartments, etc., all have little quirks which we will not discussed here.)

Note: (A) Ministers or members of the uniformed services that receive a housing allowance that is not taxable can still deduct their home mortgage interest. B) If your client qualifies for mortgage assistance payments for lower-income families under section 235 of the National Housing Act, part or all of the interest on their mortgage may be paid for them. They cannot deduct the interest that is paid for them. C) If a divorce or separation agreement requires your client or their spouse or former spouse to pay home mortgage interest on a home owned by both of them, the payment of interest may be alimony. See the discussion of Payments for jointly-owned home under Alimony in Publication 504, Divorced or Separated Individuals.

In order for mortgage interest to be deductible not only must your client file Form 1040 and itemize deductions on Schedule A, your client must be legally liable for the loan. They cannot deduct payments they make for someone else if they are not legally liable to make them. There has to be an intention that the loan be repaid, that there is a true debtor-creditor relationship, and the mortgage must be a secured debt on a qualified home. The next question for your client is will they take the Standard Deduction or will they itemize? They can't do both, in order to make an informed decision they need to determine if their itemized deductions exceed the standard deduction for their filing status.

While there are other expenses that can be itemized on Schedule A, like medical expenses in excess of 7.5% of AGI, or charitable contributions, or miscellaneous expenses in excess of 2% of AGI, etc., our focus will remain on the only two homeownership related expenses that are currently deductible – applicable real estate taxes and qualified mortgage interest.

Let's take a moment and define real estate taxes and qualified mortgage interest.

Real Estate Taxes – those taxes actually paid at closing or settlement or imposed on your client by a taxing authority and paid directly or through an escrow account during the applicable year. The best source for this information is the tax bill itself.

Here's an important and practical real estate tax point – For federal income tax purposes, the seller of the property is treated as paying the property taxes up to, but not including, the date of sale. The buyer is treated as paying the taxes beginning with the date of sale. This date and information can generally be found by looking at the settlement statement your client received at closing. This rule applies even if the buyer or seller paid the full amount at closing, each person can deduct their applicable share. This rule does not apply (between buyer and seller) if the taxes were delinquent, then the amount would be added to the cost basis of the home. This could be a valuable negotiating point, particularly since the seller could have already paid the property taxes for the year, so they wouldn't necessarily miss the money, but it may enhance and facilitate an otherwise stalled sale.

Any sales tax imposed on the purchase of the house can be deducted if the client elects to deduct state and local general sales taxes instead of state and local income taxes.

Qualified Mortgage Interest – The general rule is that if all of your mortgages fit into one or more of the following three categories at all times during the year, you can deduct all of the interest on those mortgages: (1) grand fathered debt, (2) home receive debt, and (3) home equity debt. (If any one mortgage fits into more than one category, add the debt that fits in each category to the other debt in the same category.)

Since you are providing mortgage planning advice and not general tax advice what is and isn't part of the homeowner's cost basis isn't your focus. Cost basis is the amount that constitutes what your home cost you. In practical terms, it would be similar to the concept of price paid for the home. "When it comes to owning a home not only will you pay the price, but you will pay the costs, and most costs of homeownership are not deductible, like they are with investment property." There is no current deduction for homeowner's insurance premiums, FHA or mortgage insurance premiums, fire, comprehensive or title insurance, utilities, most settlement costs, transfer taxes, depreciation of the home, or principal paid on a mortgage.

Now, let's further define the three categories of mortgage debt that meet the requirements of qualified mortgage interest.

Grand fathered debt – is mortgage debt taken out on a primary or second home on or before October 14, 1987, or if such a mortgage is refinanced, it may qualify as grandfathered debt. To qualify, it must have been secured by a qualified home on October 13, 1987, and at all times after that date. How the proceed were used does not matter. Grandfathered debt is not limited. All of the interest paid on grandfathered debt is fully deductible home mortgage interest. However, the amount of grandfathered debt reduces the $1 million limit for home acquisition debt and the limit based on the home's fair market value for home equity debt.

Home receive debt – Mortgages taken out after October 13, 1987, to buy, build, or improve a principal or second residence, but only if throughout the year these mortgages plus any grandfathered debt totaled $1 million or less ($500,000 or less if married filing separately).

Home equity debt – Mortgages took out after October 13, 1987, other than to buy, build, or improve a a primary or secondary residence, but only if throughout the year these mortgages totaled $100,000 or less ($50,000 or less if married filing separately) and totalled no more than the fair market value of the home reduced by grand fathered debt and home aquistion debt.

As you can see, there are two limiting conditions on the mortgage interest deduction, the first one has to do with the size of the mortgage and the second has to do with the category under which the debt fits. Mortgage interest is limited to the first million dollars of debt ($500,000 if married filing separately) and to the categories described above.

To determine the amount of mortgage interest your client has look at the Form 1098 – otherwise known as the mortgage interest statement. Your client should receive this form or a similar statement from the mortgage holder if they had $600 or more of mortgage interest (including certain points) during the year on any one mortgage. Your client will receive the statement if they pay interest to a person (including a financial institution or cooperative housing corporation) in the course of that person's trade or business. A governmental unit is a person for purposes of furnishing the statement. The statement for each year should be sent to your client by January 31 of the following year. A copy of this form will also be sent to the IRS. The statement will show the total interest your client paid during the year. If your client purchased a main home during the year, it also will show the deductible points paid during the year, including seller-paid points. However, it should not show any interest that was paid for your client by a government agency. As a general rule, Form 1098 will include only points that you can fully deduct in the year paid. However, certain points not included on Form 1098 may also be deductible, either in the year paid or over the life of the loan. You should seek the advice of an income tax advisor for additional information.

With rental property you can dedcut the normal and necessary expense of managing, conserving and maintaining while it is vacant, rented or pending sale including depreciation. Repairs are deductible – they don't add value or extend the useful life of the property. Improvements are capitalized. Other expenses you can deduct include: advertising, cleaning and maintenance, utilities, insurance, taxes, interest, points, commissions, tax return preparation fees, travel expenses, rental payments, and local transportation expenses.

There are a couple of myths related to the mortgage interest deduction that we will address here.

Myth 1 – Prepaying your January interest in December to increase the amount of your interest deduction. Although you generally pay mortgage interest in arrears, some clients maybe paying a month or two in advance. In some instances there maybe some prepaid interest on Form 1098. For example, if your client prepaid interest in one calendar year that accrued in full by January 15, 2007, this prepaid interest may be included in box 1 of Form 1098. However, they cannot deduct the prepaid amount for January 2007 in 2006. You will have to figure the interest that accrued for 2006 and subtract it from the amount in box 1. You will include the interest for January 2007 with other interest you pay for 2007.

Myth 2 – Your client can liquefy their home equity and invest in securities or certificates that produce tax-free income and elect to deduct the associated mortgage interest. If your client uses mortgage proceeds to invest in tax-exempt securities, they <u>cannot</u> deduct the home mortgage interest on grandfathered debt or home equity debt if the proceeds are used to buy securities or certificates that produce tax-free income.

As a QMP™ professional, you may be called upon to accurately calcuate the mortgage interest deduction because consumers commonly ask about the tax savings of having a mortgage. More than likely the answer given by most practititioners is wrong. There are many calculations that are so over simplified that the answer produced is inaccurate. The results tend to overstate the tax benefits associated with homeownership. Possibly in an attempt to simplify the calculation or maybe in an attempt to sell a mortgage or a larger mortgage, typically missing from the equation is the impact of the standard tax deduction. It's the missing link.

In the zest to sell the immediate benefits of a home or a mortgage, the fact that a consumer can experience tax savings (depending on their situation) is overstated and improperly demonstrated so that it overstates the estimated tax savings. The big fallacy is a direct result of ignoring the standard tax deduction. The fact is the interest deduction is not a consideration when purchasing a home unless the borrower's total deductions exceed the standard deductions such that the borrower is able to itemize for tax purposes. The standard deduction varies by income tax filing status.

Ignoring the standard deduction is incorrect because (1) not everyone uses itemized deductions on their tax return, even with mortgage interest, literally millions of mortgagors still fall short of exceeding the standard deduction, (2) mortgage interest may not result in any tax savings if itemized deductions do not exceed the standard deduction and (3) it is only the amount by which the itemized deductions exceed the standard deduction that we start to receive any tax savings and then it is a function of your marginal tax rate.

Usually the tax savings are estimated as the difference between the applicable income taxes on adjusted gross income with and without the mortgage interest deduction.

$$(AGI \times MTR) - ((AGI - MI) \times MTR) = \text{Tax Savings}$$

AGI = Adjusted gross income

MTR = Marginal tax rate

MI = Mortgage interest

If tax savings are calculated in this manner it assumes that the consumer is in a position to itemize already. However, unless the total deductions, including mortgage interest, exceed the standard deduction for the relevant tax filing status, the consumer probably does not itemize. And if the consumer does not have enough deductions to itemize, then there are no tax savings resulting from mortgage interest or any other allowable deduction. It is only to the extent that the mortgage interest deduction impacts the itemized deductions that the consumer starts to derive tax savings.

According to IRS data, only 27.89% of all tax returns filed in 2001 had a mortgage interest deduction and the average amount of interest claimed was $9,102.

Be careful to compare accurately the difference in expected itemized tax deductions versus the standard deduction when comparing the front-end benefits.

Here are simple formulas:

(Total Itemized Deductions – Standard Deduction) X Marginal Tax Rate = Tax Savings

or if the consumer currently itemizes before having a mortgage:

(Total Itemized Deductions with the Mortgage Interest Deduction – Total Itemized Deductions without the Mortgage Interest Deduction) X Effective Tax Rate = Tax Savings from Mortgage Interest Deduction.

<u>Mortgage Prepayment Equivalent Yield™ (MPEY) Calculation</u>

Homeowners often consider the benefits of pulling equity out of the home to make investments or divert discretionary funds towards investments rather than applying those funds toward prepaying the mortgage. The MPEY™ calculation, as provided in Mortgage Based™ Financial Planning, provides an objective way to make those type decisions. The focus of the MPEY™ calculation is not just on the tax treatment of the mortgage or even the alternative investment, but in recognizing the trichotomy of a mortgaged home. As was stated previously in this book, a mortgaged home can be considered an investment, a physical asset, and a financial liability. We must recognize all sides.

The MPEY™ calculation results in a value that can be determined for any homeowner or prospective homeowner based on their personal situation. The calculation is based on comparing the taxpayer's financial situation with and without a mortgage to investment options, and determining which direction the benefits flow by comparing any loss or gain in tax benefits, any loss or gain in real cash flow, and recognizing either the appropriate appraised or stated value of the property.

The MPEY™ calculation results in a value that can be used as a comparison to the projected rate of return of any investment. It provides the rate above which an investment must earn before it beats the financial benefits of prepaying the mortgage and is most easily illustrated in situations involving the now classic decisions of whether to invest an amount equal to the outstanding (current) mortgage balance or pay-off the mortgage in a lump sum. The MPEY™ calculation demonstrates a working understanding of both the Mortgage Portfolio™ Theory and the Mortgage Optimization™ Theory and could be used as a standard of suitability in financial planning and in recommending or selling investment products.

How does the MPEY™ calculation recognize the trichotomy of the home? The liability side of the mortgage is recognized in the improved cash flow resulting from eliminating the mortgage and the asset side of the mortgaged property is recognized in the tax-free rental value of the property (TFRV). The MPEY™ calculation illustrates the need to service the mortgage while awaiting a potential return and also recognizes that income taxes must be paid on investment income unless the funds are invested in tax-free instruments. Whereas, some people will say that the equity in a home has a zero rate of return or that the home equity is an idle asset, the MPEY™ calculation gives equity a quantifiable value.

The cost of paying the interest must also be considered. The money used to pay the mortgage interest comes from somewhere: job earnings, interest income, etc. How much has to be earned to end up with enough to pay the interest in the first place? We must recognize at a minimum the costs of the mortgage interest deduction.

The benefit of the mortgage interest deduction is oversold, over emphasized and over calculated relative to a benefit that generally doesn't get honorably mentioned by academics, practitioners, bankers or the President's Commission on Tax Reform of 2005. Generally, the value of the mortgage interest deduction pales in comparison to the tax free-rental value. The tax-free rental value is the fair market rental value of a property minus the actual expenses paid or incurred for occupying the property as a primary residence. The tax-free rental value and the additional cash flow resulting from the elimination of the mortgage are typically many times greater than the mortgage interest deduction. This concept is presented in greater detail in the course on Mortgage Based™ Financial Planning.

What does $100 of mortgage interest actually cost?

	1	*2*	*3*	*4*
To Pay $100 In Interest	Earned W-2	Interest Income	Tax Free Int.	LT Capital Gain
	$100.00	$100.00	$100.00	$100.00
On the Job Expenses	$0.00	0	0	0
State & Local Taxes	$0.00	0	0	0
Social Security Taxes	$11.61	0	0	0
Medicare Taxes	$2.20	0	0	0
Income Taxes	$37.94	$33.33	$0.00	$17.65
Gross Earnings	$151.75	$133.33	$100.00	$117.65

The above example is based upon a person in the 25% marginal tax bracket. Whether or not the mortgage interest results in tax savings remains a function of the relevant filing status and total itemized deductions versus the standard deduction. Column one shows how much W-2 income has to be earned in order to net enough money to pay the $100 in mortgage interest.

Column two and three show how much income is needed from interest income or tax-free income in order to pay the $100 in mortgage interest. Column four is based upon a long-term capital gain rate of 15%.

The critical question is what is the source of funds used to pay the interest? Did it come from wages and salaries, interest, tax-exempt interest, ordinary dividends, etc. The source of the income impacts the actual cost of funds.

Summary

By performing Mortgage Fundamental™ Analysis and Mortgage Technical™ Analysis, the QMP™ professional can help the consumer determine the suitability of their mortgage decisions from mortgage loan program selection to prepayment and investment choices. When it comes to investment choices, the MPEY™ calculation takes the guesswork out of the question of whether to prepay the mortgage in a lump sum or invest those funds elsewhere.

As a professional, you are solely responsible for the content of your recommendations, and by performing these kinds of objective analyses you will be ready to do so and you will have documentation to back you up.

Chapter 6

Plan Development & Communicating Findings
- Putting It All Together & Telling Them What You Know -

"True eloquence, indeed, does not consist in speech. It cannot be brought from far. Labor and learning may toil for it, but they will toil in vain. Words and phrases may be marshalled in every way, but they cannot compass it. It must exist in the man, in the subject, and in the occasion."

- Daniel Webster -

Ongoing development and product innovation creates a barrage of new mortgage products that provide consumers with increased loan program choices, but it has also increased the complexity of the loan decision process. The loan options and loan disclosures that must be quickly evaluated by consumers puts them in a vulnerable position and when it comes to refinancing, consideration must be given to more than just rate. For example, in a refinance, the new term along with other relevant factors must be considered in order to determine if refinancing will result in cost savings or if it will actually increase the total cost of ownership. An upcoming example will demonstrate this point.

Consumers generally lack sufficient knowledge to decipher the immediate impact of the decisions they must make, not to mention how these decisions will impact their abilities to fulfill other financial responsibilities and goals, including financial independence. As a QMP™ professional, you should be able to help the consumer determine the most suitable mortgage options for them given their particular circumstances, financial goals and objectives.

For the QMP™ professional, mortgage plan development is simply a matter of putting together all the quantitative and qualitative facts you've gathered regarding the client with your findings following your analyses and evaluations of that data. In all fairness to the client and the integrity of your practice, it is best to be forthright in the disclosure of your review and findings. Unethical business practices may lead to a one-time fee, if that, but the damage to your business reputation may linger indefinitely. Client retention and client referrals stem from the client's sense of your professionalism, honesty and fair play.

Following the process as outlined in this book, you've examined the client's personal situation, financial resources, financial objectives and financial problems in a comprehensive manner. Therefore, the result will be the development of an impartial, integrated plan to best utilize client resources to meet the client's objectives and to solve real client problems, while introducing and employing a process that recognizes the significance that housing, and any associated debt, play in the realization of client (short-term and long-term) life goals and objectives.

Being able to consult with a QMP™ professional is a practice that's long over due since most people have no specific written financial objective in relation to their home. They are just happy to have found a home that they liked and to have qualified for the mortgage. That was the financial objective. Mortgage decisions are often made without regard to any specific overall financial objective and thus there is no basis for determining their financial success. Undoubtedly, the time to ask questions to determine how the mortgage decision will impact the consumer's financial future is prior to the consumer signing the loan application.

As part of a mortgage plan of action you can help consumers with decisions such as:

> How to develop a financial plan that helps them to manage and monitor their mortgage?

> How to implement a plan to pay off their mortgage in their timeframe and relative to their resources?

Should a mortgagor put more toward paying off their mortgage (if so, how much more) or should they invest those funds elsewhere (if the client has discretionary funds)?

When does a client's financial goals necessitate a change in mortgage terms?

What are the pros and cons of various mortgage programs?

When is a thirty-year, fifteen-year, or adjustable rate mortgage appropriate?

You can advise consumers on factors, beyond rate, that they should considered in evaluating their financing options.

You can advise consumers as to when and why loan programs such as interest only are suitable.

You can advise consumers regarding their particular financing options considering the strength of credit, employment, availability of documentation, etc.

You can analyze and compare good faith estimates providing consumers with an unbiased opinion on this loan cost disclosure. (Keep in mind that if you are not a mortgage broker or loan officer, in some states you cannot negotiate a loan for your client.)

You can show consumers how their mortgage decisions impact their overall financial plans.

Keep in mind that the vale you add is your ability to provide client appropriate specific advice that can save the client many times the fee charged, avoiding costly financial mistakes by applying general rules of thumb that don't necessarily apply to your client.

There are some common mistakes mortgagors make that you should look out for such as:

- Thinking that their mortgage decisions are independent of other financial planning decisions;
- Maximizing the debt-to-income ratios when applying for a mortgage;
- Ignoring known and anticipated new debts, expenses or expected reductions in income when calculating the debt-to-income ratio;
- Pulling equity out of the home for reasons other than financial hardship or for making improvements that increase the value of the property;
- Not shortening the timeline for repaying the mortgage and not recognizing the benefits of doing so;
- Over valuing the mortgage interest deduction;
- Believing that a debt free home is an idle asset, while failing to recognize the tax-free status of a property's fair rental value, the value of a reduced cash flow requirement or the fact that when all is said and done, everybody's got to live somewhere; and
- Not recognizing the differences between a tax deduction, tax deferral, a tax exemption and a tax credit.

With that in mind, let's look at the scenario below regarding the mortgagor's decision to refinance. It shows that refinancing based on a decrease in rate may not always result in the best long-term solution and that it's easy for consumers to confuse cost savings with monthly cash flow.

> Joe Median started out with a mortgage of $69,000 at 8.4% fixed for 30 years with a P&I payment of $525.67.
>
> He refinanced the remaining balance of $61,017 after 10 years. Joe obtained a new 30-year loan with a fixed rate of 6.4% and paid zero closing costs.
>
> Joe lowered his payment to $381.66 or by $144.01 (27.3%).
>
> Joe cut his interest rate by 200 basis points or 24% below his previous rate and Joe reduced his itemized interest by 25%, thus raising the bar for the amount required to take advantage of itemization on his tax return.
>
> How much in mortgage savings did Joe experience over the life of these mortgages?
>
> During the first ten years Joe paid $63,080.40 in mortgage payments ($525.67 X 120 months).

After refinancing, Joe paid a total of $137,397.60 over the new thirty-year period.

By the end of the total mortgage period, Joe has paid $200,478. Remember the original loan was for $69,000.

If Joe had not refinanced, but had continued to pay the 8.4% rate for the entire 30-year period, Joe would have paid a total of $189,237.

In this scenario, refinancing ended up costing Joe $11,241 more money over the life of the loans ($200,478 - $189,237), without any regard to any possible tax deduction.

How can this be if Joe reduced his interest rate by 200 basis points?

Joe did something that is commonly done by many consumers who refinance. Joe opted for a new 30-year mortgage period, which ended up being a costly decision.

If Joe had opted for a twenty-year loan to maintain a thirty-year total mortgage period, the outcome would have been different.

Refinancing for a twenty-year period at a fixed rate of 6.4% would have decreased Joe's payment to $451.34. Over the twenty-year period Joe would have paid $108,321.60. Recognizing the payments Joe made during the first ten years, Joe would have paid a total of $171,402.20 over the life of the mortgages ($108,321.60 + $63,080.60).

In this instance, as a result of the refinance, Joe would have realized mortgage savings of $17,835 ($189,237 - $171,402).

Now let's go one step further.

Assume Joe opted to continue to make a payment in line with his previous mortgage payment of $525.

By doing this Joe can decrease the term of the new mortgage to fifteen years. Reducing the term of the new mortgage to fifteen years requires a new payment of $528.17 or $2.50 more per month than the original payment.

After fifteen years, Joe will have paid $95,070.70 for the new mortgage.

Joe will have reduced the total mortgage period to twenty-five years, ten years for the original mortgage and fifteen years for the refinance.

The total payments over the twenty-five year period would be $158,151.20 ($95,070.60 + $63,080.60).

The savings resulting from the refinance would be $31,086 ($189,237 - $158,151).

Chart of Joe's Refinance Options

	Original Mortgage	Refinance Over 30 Years	Refinance Over 20 Years	Refinance Over 15 Years
Loan Amount	$69,000	$61,017	$61,017	$61,017
Term	30	30	20	15
Rate	8.4%	6.4%	6.4%	6.4%
Payment	$525.67	$381.66	$451.34	$528.17
Total Paid Over Term	$189.237	$137,397	$108,321	$95,070
Add Amount Paid on Original Term		$63,081	$63,081	$63,081
Total Paid Over Life of Both Mortgages		$200,478	$171,402	$158,151
Mortgage Savings (Cost)		($11,241)	$17,835	$31,086

As you can see, the decision to refinance requires more consideration than just rate and the amount of closing costs.

In our example, the change in rate was held constant and the closing costs were assumed to be zero.

Depending on the term of the refinancing, Joe could have ended up paying more than he would have if he had maintained his original 8.4% loan.

Just following the rule of thumb of refinancing whenever the interest rate is 2% points below where you are may not yield the desired result. Refinancing at a lower rate presents a good opportunity to produce cost savings by reducing the term of the mortgage while holding the payment to a fairly constant level.

Additionally, if Joe had opted for a 15 year term he may have been able to enjoy any rate differential between the 30 and 20 or 15 year loan terms, e.g. another .25 basis point reduction in rate or $9.93 a month, may not seem like much but $9.93 eliminates just over two years of payments (25.26 months or $9,640.73) on a 30 year term.

The same quarter point (.25% or $8.90) eliminates just over 9 months worth of payments on a twenty-year term (9.08 months or $4,098.17) and over 4 (4.6 months or $2,426.56) of payments on a 15-year loan with $8.32 (.25% reduction) a month applied toward principal.

The average savings amounts to $5,388 or over 12.98 months of payments from an average of $9.05 a month. Who's encouraging you to save $9.05 a month or 30 cents a day with contractually guaranteed results? Who can you encourage?

As far as the tax savings are concerned, there would be no tax implications from Joe Median's refinance given his tax filing status of married filing jointly. Joe's itemized deductions did not exceed the standard deduction either before or after the refinance.

Think about what's unique about your client's situation?

Now let's look at a different scenario.

In this scenario we will look at the impact of using other people's money (OPM) or leverage.

In this instance, the difference between Joe Median's down payment and the purchase price of his house is going to be borrowed from the mortgage company.

Joe Median is considering the purchase of a new home as a primary residence. Joe is considering whether to make a down payment of 10%, 20% or 100% (an all cash transaction).

Joe contracts to purchase the house for $100,000.

In the example, we are going to compare an all cash transaction with a 10% and 20% down payment.

Leverage Scenario Table 1

	A	B	C
	10% Down	**20% down**	**100% down**
Purchase Price	$100,000	$100,000	$100,000
Down Payment	-$10,000	-$20,000	-$100,000
Amount Financed	$90,000	$80,000	$0

The amount of leverage is determined by comparing the amount of debt to the amount of equity. In the above example, the amount of leverage is 90%, 80% and zero, respectively.

Leverage can be very attractive depending on how you look at it. The idea behind leverage is that you get to control a larger asset with a smaller amount of equity.

Leverage works well in the lives of millions of American for personal and business reasons. However, leverage is better applied to business and investments than items used for personal consumption. The primary reason is the basic economic principle revolving around the idea that there is no such thing as a free lunch and you have to pay for it with interest.

In the above example, Joe can control a piece of property worth $100,000 with as little as $10,000 down and a mortgage. If he paid cash for the property, he would have no leverage.

There are those in the financial community who believe that not taking advantage of leverage is a real waste. They will tell you that the consumer is wasting away an asset, an asset that could be working for them in an investment. So they will tell the consumer that the idea of even considering paying cash for such a large purchase is ridiculous and that they will lose out on the mortgage interest deduction, and some will even suggest that the person doesn't understand the economic concept of opportunity costs.

In this next scenario, let's assume that the property appreciates at a rate of 5% per year.

If that were the case, then over five years the property would have a value as displayed below.

Leverage Scenario **Table 2 Appreciation**

	A	B	C
	5% Appreciation per year		
Initial Value	$100,000	$100,000	$100,000
Year One	$105,000	$105,000	$105,000
Year Two	$110,250	$110,250	$110,250
Year Three	$115,763	$115,763	$115,763
Year Four	$121,551	$121,551	$121,551
Year Five	$127,628	$127,628	$127,628

The rate of appreciation is applied equally to all three scenarios. It was not determined by the amount of leverage on the property.

Now, assume that Joe decides to sell the property. Let's take a look at the numbers.

Joe purchased the property for $100,000, and sells the property five years later for $127,628.

The value over the purchase price is $27,628 in each scenario.

However, in Column A, Joe put down $10,000 and earned $27,628 (276% over five years or 55.2% per year return).

In Column B, Joe put down $20,000 and earned the same $27,628 (138.1% over five years or 27.62% per year).

In Column C, Joe put down $100,000 and still earned $27,628 (27.62% over five years or 5.52% per year).

As you can see, the return was 10 times greater in Column A than in Column C.

At this point, the idea of leverage is probably looking good.

But, before proclaiming leverage as the victor, consider the impact of the mortgage.

Leverage Scenario Table 3 - Mortgage

	A	B	C
	Loan - Interest Only @ 7%		
Initial Loan Amount	$90,000	$80,000	$0
Year One	$6,300	$5,600	$0
Year Two	$6,300	$5,600	$0
Year Three	$6,300	$5,600	$0
Year Four	$6,300	$5,600	$0
Year Five	$6,300	$5,600	$0
Totals over 5 years	$31,500	$28,000	$0

In arriving at the true rate of return, we have to take the payments on the mortgage into account.

The mortgages in Columns A and B assume an interest-only loan at 7%.

Column A shows that the $90,000 mortgage required payments totaling $31,500 over the five year period.

Column B shows that the $80,000 mortgage required payments totaling $28,000 over the five year period.

There was no mortgage in Column C.

Once you consider the payments made on the mortgage, the numbers are not as appealing.

The return in Column A becomes (7.74%).

The return in Column B becomes (.372).

And the return in Column C remains 5.52%.

Adjusted Gross Return

	A	B	C
	Determining The Gain		
Sales Price	$127,628	$127,628	$127,628
Outstanding Loan Balance	-$90,000	-$80,000	$0
Interest Charges	-$31,500	-$28,000	$0
Initial Investment/Down	-$10,000	-$20,000	-$100,000
Net Gain/ Loss	-$3,872	-$372	$27,628
Average / Year	-$774	-$74	$5,526
Average Return Per Yr.	-7.744%	-0.372%	5.526%

In reviewing the use of OPM, we see that as it relates to residential property, it can be a little costly to overlook the facts, but let's review both the pros and cons:

Pros

- Joe had control and possession of the property when he wanted it even though he didn't pay the full purchase price up front.

- Joe can live in the property and enjoy all the benefits of homeownership.

- Joe gets to will the property to anyone he wants.

- Joe can buy a life insurance policy and for a few dollars per thousand dollars of coverage he can guarantee income tax-free dollars that can be used by Joe's designated beneficiary to pay the mortgage off in the event of his untimely demise.

- Joe could decide on the type of loan and the kind of terms that appeal to him given his mortgage mission and strategy statements.

- Joe decided, for purposes of monthly cash flow, that he wanted an interest-only loan, but he wanted the certainty of knowing that his interest rate wouldn't change during the time he planned to own the property.

- Joe planned to live in the house five years, but weighed the pros and cons of both the five and seven year adjustable rates and decided to put a little cushion in there and closed on the 7 year interest-only adjustable loan. The difference in rate was .25 points and he felt it was worth the extra $225 on the $90,000 loan and $200 a year on the $80,000 loan.

- Joe maintained his cash flow and kept his payment to a minimum with the interest-only loan.

Cons

- Joe had monthly payments in addition to coming up with the down payment.

- Joe's total itemized deductions didn't exceed the standard deduction so there were no additional tax benefits associated with the mortgage.

- Joe incurred additional costs associated with the loan, e.g., appraisal, underwriting fees, etc.

Let's look at a scenario where Joe Median has discretionary funds of $149 per month and is considering whether to invest the $149 at a 10% rate of return and then apply the funds to the mortgage, to directly apply the funds to his mortgage, or to spending the discretionary funds. This scenario assumes that the mortgage has no prepayment penalty.

Original Mortgage Amount of $69,000
30-Year Fixed Rate at 8.4%

	Column # 1	Column #2	Column # 3
	30-Yr Mortgage at 8.4% Fixed Rate Amortized Over Term	**$149 Invested Monthly at 10% in a side fund and then applied to the mortgage balance**	**$149 Applied Directly to Prepay the mortgage balance**
	Mortgage Balance	Mortgage Balance	Mortgage Balance
Year			
1	$68,468	$66,607	$66,609
5	$65,831	$54,666	$54,712
7	$64,144	$46,960	$47,099
10	$61,017	$32,587	$32,999
12	$58,452	$20,714	$21,428
15	$53,701	$1426 Credit Balance	$0
20	$42,581	No Mortgage	No Mortgage
25	$25,682	No Mortgage	No Mortgage
30	$0	No Mortgage	No Mortgage

Column one assumes payments were made as scheduled and no extra payments were made. There is no impact on the mortgage because the money was spent elsewhere.

Column two assumes **no commissions** were paid on the investment and **no taxes** were paid on the investment proceeds. However, a 1.25% management fee is assumed.

Column three requires **no management fee**, **no commissions paid on the additional payments**, and **no taxes payable on the mortgage savings**. It requires **no side account or associated risks**.

In Column one, the mortgage is paid off in thirty years as scheduled.

In Column two, the mortgage is paid off in fifteen years with an over payment of $1,426.

In Column three, the mortgage is paid off in fifteen years.

Obviously, the assumptions in Column two are not realistic. Depending on the investment, the return may not be at a stable 10% as assumed and it may be impossible to avoid taxes. There are always either commissions, surrender charges, maintenance fees, management fees, 12b(1) fees, or other assessments or fees for making an investment, etc.

As you can see from the scenarios presented here, the best plan of action will differ based on each client's circumstances and there may be no hard and fast rules that can be applied uniformly to all clients. It's imperative that individuals look at their situation, circumstances, facts, guarantees, assumptions and **risks** individually. These scenarios also show that the actual outcome may differ significantly from what you suspect or may even expect, which is why it's necessary as a professional not to prejudge the situation.

Communicating Your Findings

Having documented your findings and recommendations you've got tangible evidence of what you know about the client's situation. It should be clear from your documentation that you took an objective approach that considered both quantitative and qualitative client based data. The mortgage plan you've developed should include summaries of the results of your Mortgage Fundamental Analysis™ and your Mortgage Technical Analysis™.

The mission statement and strategy statement gave the client an opportunity to play an active role in the plan development. The fact that the plan reflects the client's statements demonstrates that you developed the plan based on an interactive process. Additionally, seeing their statements within the plan creates a greater commitment on the part of the client to plan implementation. Jeffrey Kelvin and William Ruckstuhl noted in *Financial Planning Applications* that, "The best decisions are those made by the person or persons involved after they have been given sufficient information to allow them to make an informed selection from several known alternatives. The planner must learn to function within this framework, learning to accept and even to encourage clients' questioning of planning recommendations."[16] However, being that you can't force a client to accept your recommendation, even if it is the most suitable, you will have "facts" in the form of the client's mission statement and strategy statement, to document the client's decision. The mortgage plan should also document that you provided full and fair disclosure of all material matters to your client.

The written mortgage plan should provide understandable action steps for the client of the QMP™ professional's recommendations along with any viable alternatives that reflect the client's stated objectives and goals. The QMP™ professional should develop a basic mortgage plan format (presentation of an essential set of information and recommendations) that is used consistently from client to client to avoid claims that the plan presentation and format are arbitrary and capricious.

You should speak clearly, positively and audibly as you communicate your findings. Explain your recommendations in common language, limiting your use of industry jargon and defining any jargon that can't be avoided. Your body language is also important. It should convey a sense of confidence and competence. If you are unsure about your recommendations, your oral expression and body language will communicate that. Rather than trying to pass off an ill-prepared plan, it's better to first review your work and talk your recommendations over with another mortgage planner before presenting the plan to your client.

Remember you've got to tell your clients not only what they want to know, but also what they need to know in order to make intelligent mortgage and financial decisions. You had a good starting point, your client's mission and a strategy they found reasonable to follow. Your recommendations should be the most appropriate course of action based on the best information available at the time.

Summary

Putting together all the quantitative and qualitative facts you've gathered regarding the client along with your findings based on your analyses and evaluations of that data is what mortgage plan development is all about. Some of your recommendations will likely challenge many of your client's ingrained yet inaccurate beliefs and open their minds to new possibilities.

It is best to be forthright in the disclosure of your review and findings even if your recommendations include concepts and ideas that are new and different to your client. Your documentation will show that you took an objective approach that considered both quantitative and qualitative client based data not to mention that you followed an interactive process that included the client's self-written mission and strategy statements.

Chapter 7

Plan Implementation - Putting The Plan Into Action -

"There are two things to aim at in life; first to get what you want, and after that to enjoy it. Only the wisest of mankind has achieved the second."

- Logan Pearsall Smith -

Plan implementation is an interactive step whereby the QMP™ professional coordinates or manages the client's execution of the provided recommendations. The QMP™ professional and the client must agree on the implementation responsibilities and the client should revise his or her mission statement and strategy statement as appropriate based on the QMP™ professional's recommendations. Your job is to help the client to use effective mortgage planning techniques to reach their target goal and to do so in a professional and ethical manner, providing full and fair disclosure of identified options and material matters that should be considered in choosing the most suitable option.

If a new mortgage is required, the QMP™ professional may guide the client in shopping for a loan program that is inline with the mortgage plan. You are not acting as a negotiator, but as an independent mortgage evaluator. In shopping, you must remind your client to make sure they are comparing comparable loan products.

For the best shopping, your client should get good faith estimates from at least one of each of the following: a bank, a credit union and a broker. A credit union has competitive advantages over other lenders and can pass their cost savings on to their members. And generally, the profit margins on the loan products of a credit union are set lower than those of a bank. Be aware of any competitive advantages various lenders have. For example, the credit union has a competitive advantage of not being subject to the intangible tax, which other lenders may pass on to the borrower, and there could be certain advantages in refinancing with the same lender, such as the case with a streamline refinance where the traditional guidelines, paperwork and process don't necessarily apply to obtaining lower rates or payments, taking cash-out or removing Mortgage Insurance.

On average, one may expect better pricing from a credit union over other lenders due to the fact that it's member owned. One disadvantage to a credit union is that it may not have the diversity of loan products offered by other lenders.

Whereas lenders have to offer the same rate to borrowers who meet the set of criteria for the loan product, brokers have more flexibility and can negotiate a more competitive rate. Knowing that a broker has the greatest flexibility in pricing can be used to your advantage.

For example, you could have your client take the good faith estimate (GFE) obtained from the credit unions and banks and have the broker compete against that GFE. Of course you would want to deal with a reliable, reputable entity that will actually follow through and not just lowball the costs with no intent of actually honoring the estimate. The mortgage originator should then be willing to lock the rate and efficiently process the loan to a timely close.

In this information age, consumers often look to the Internet as the ultimate source for answers to all of their inquiries. Sometimes it's not so much that information is not available, it's having enough time to plow through it to differentiate between relevant information and rubbish, and then knowing what to do with it. Many companies offer mortgages over the Internet. It's often been noted that growth in these types of services may be a manifestation of consumers' frustrations in obtaining mortgages through more traditional channels and/or it maybe a product of our hectic lifestyles and the desire for greater convenience. We want it quick and we want it cheap, but at what sacrifice?

As a QMP™ professional, you can assist consumers in analyzing the impacts of a new mortgage on their overall financial plans, determining the suitability of available mortgage options, evaluating good faith estimates, or reviewing their existing mortgage to make sure that the loan features are still consistent with their financial plans and objectives. By evaluating the client's good faith estimate, you are providing a second opinion.

You can continue to work with the client throughout the mortgage transaction to assess and to help explain the available loan programs being considered by the client. You may also accompany the client to closing to make sure that the final paperwork is consistent with the preliminary documents and cost disclosures previously provided to the client.

When utilizing the services of a QMP™ professional, the consumer also creates a self-policing force within the mortgage industry for the benefit of all consumers without more government regulation. Through utilizing the principals and concepts put forth in this book, the QMP™ professional can help the consumer assess the risk and rewards associated with having, holding and retiring a mortgage on their primary residence.

In developing a defensive investment portfolio position for the client, your recommendation will include a repayment strategy to prepay the mortgage. Being that any prepayments reduce the amount of interest charged on the outstanding balance, it may be possible to structure the prepayments of your client's mortgage such that it is not necessary to incur the expense of refinancing in order to enjoy the cost savings from prepaying the mortgage.

Coordinating or managing the client's implementation of the mortgage plan is critical to the process to ensure that the details of the plan are not lost to the client. It is imperative that the plan is fully and properly implemented in order for there to be an immediate and/or long-term positive impact on the client's quality of life. What is the plan truly worth if it's never implemented?

The client may pay for the plan after you have delivered your recommendations, however, the mortgage planning process is not over and your job is not yet complete.

Summary

Implementing the plan is an interactive step whereby you coordinate or manage the client's execution of your recommendations. You and your client should come to an understanding on who is responsible for what in getting the plan implemented. At this point, your job is to help the client use effective mortgage planning techniques to reach their target goal. In doing so, you should provide full and fair disclosure of identified options and material matters that should be considered in choosing the most suitable option. Most likely your client will continue to rely on you for guidance during the implementation phase. If a new mortgage is part of the plan, make sure your client is aware that the mortgage planning engagement has concluded before you put your sales hat on.

Chapter 8

Monitoring A Mortgage Plan
- Looking Back Every Now & Then -

"All great masters are chiefly distinguished by the power of adding a second, a third, and perhaps a fourth step in a continuous line. Many a man has taken the first step. With every additional step you enhance immensely the value of your first."

- Ralph Waldo Emerson -

Monitoring the mortgage plan provides an opportunity for you to stay in close touch with your clients. If not provided for in your mortgage planning letter of engagement, you and your client should sign a new engagement letter to establish the parameters of the review so that it can be readily determined whether or not the client's expectations are met. It is best if the review is conducted face-to-face, however, it can be conducted by telephone or other means.

This annual (quarterly, monthly) checkup is when the client gets to see and hear how managing their mortgage has brought them closer to realizing their mortgage objectives. This process represents a renewal of the client's commitment to doing just that and it's where you get to provide much needed praise and positive reinforcement. The review does not have to be a costly and protracted process, but it's meant to help keep the client on track.

The review should start with an evaluation of the progress the client has made since the last review. For this you can compare the mortgage balance at the beginning and end of the period, exam the client's log of mortgage prepayments, calculate the average prepayment amount, note your observations regarding particular months or times of the year when the largest prepayments are made, and highlight other efforts that the client made to realize their mortgage goals. You should look back at the strategies that were in place during the previous period to determine if those strategies worked as well as you thought. Strategies need to be evaluated, restructured and possibly replaced if they are not moving your client in the right direction.

An assessment of the existing mortgage should also be done. You should review with the client how their loan rate compares with current market rates, assess any changes or improvements that could be or should be made based on what's available in the market, look for improvements in the client's credit score and other aspects of their financial situation that would make refinancing on better terms a viable and cost effective option or even explore the possibilities of eliminating the mortgage all together.

The review also entails determining what changes have taken place that warrant changes in the mortgage plan or replacement of the mortgage that the client currently has. You should note changes in the client's income, marital status, dependents, expenses, and other financial requirements that would impact the mortgage plan.

During the review, the client should reevaluate their mission statement and strategy statement. The mortgage plan or plan of action should be modified, if necessary, to reflect changes in those statements.

Review with the client the portion of his/her discretionary income that is being allocated to prepaying the mortgage. You should help the client determine if there should be any change in the portion allocated or if the amount of discretionary income has increased, whether the increase should be applied to the mortgage. You should update your projection of the loan amortization based on the amount the client expects to prepay monthly over the next year.

Help your client to know their loan. Make them aware of the rate, the term and any loan features that are subject to change. Note the date of the original loan, the interest rate, the type of loan, whether there is a prepayment penalty and, if so, when it expires. If your client has an adjustable rate loan, know the particulars about when and by how much the rate can adjust and the index that it's tied to.

Re-evaluate your client's loan to value ratio. Suggest that your client find out whether their lender will let your client substitute a current appraisal in support of a new home value so that your client will know when they can eliminate the PMI; and under what conditions.

Review and re-evaluate your client's debt-to-income ratio. Don't rely on underwriting guidelines as an indicator of the appropriate debt-to-income ratio targets for your client's particular situation. The lower the debt-to-income ratio, the greater the client's chances of being on track.

Make a note of your client's new debts, expenses or expected reductions in income when calculating their debt-to-income ratio. Don't allow your clients to fool themselves regarding their true going-forward debt, expense and income levels.

No matter what debt ratio is used in underwriting, recalculate your client's debt-to-income ratio and cash reserves based on changes you know they anticipate due to increasing expenditures and income reductions they anticipate, e.g. differences in the utilities, maintenance expenses, the new furniture, etc. This way you help them avoid getting into a home and quickly realizing that they can't really afford it.

Additionally, when your client is considering refinancing, they could be costing themselves more by refinancing their mortgage, even if they are lowering their interest rate, if they don't consider the time they have put into paying their existing mortgage. Some people refinance believing that they are saving themselves lots of money, but they are really costing themselves money in the long run. They do this by continuing to opt for a thirty-year mortgage each time they refinance, which pushes out the total term of mortgaging the property. They may have reduced their interest rate by as much as several hundred basis points. However, by continuing to opt for a thirty-year mortgage rather than shortening the period to recognize the years they have already spent paying the mortgage, your client may end up paying a higher total cost for the property. Extending the total mortgage period can eat up all of the cost saving reducing the interest rate would have provided.

To help your client maximize the benefit of reducing their interest rate by refinancing, determine whether it is appropriate for them to reduce the term of the new mortgage to take into account the years they have already spent paying into the existing mortgage on the property.

Do not let your client get stuck on rate when evaluating their mortgage choices. As has been demonstrated in this book, there are factors beyond rate to consider when evaluating your client's mortgage choices and there are factors that affect the rates specifically available to them.

Also, just having your client call around asking what the rate is for the day will not result in usable information. Unless your client has disclosed enough details about their particular situation such that the rate quote is applicable to them, the rate will be meaningless.

Factors such as credit, employment, property appraised value, document type (full doc, no doc, low doc), inclusion or exclusion of escrows, loan-to-value ratio, debt-to-income ratio, cash-out, term of the loan, existence of a second mortgage, private mortgage insurance (PMI), PMI alternatives, and whether it's a purchase or refinance transaction, and the loan amount among other things, will affect the rate available to your client.

During this portion of the engagement, you not only monitor the client's progress, but you act as cheerleader. It's important to look back every now and then to make sure the client is still headed in the right direction and to make appropriate plan adjustments.

Summary

In monitoring the mortgage plan, you and your client should:

- Define monitoring responsibilities
- Review changes in personal circumstances
- Review and evaluate impact of changing tax laws
- Review and discuss changing life circumstances
- Review and/or revise mortgage mission, strategy or investment policy statement as appropriate
- Make periodic adjustments or modify recommendations as necessary

At the conclusion of the mortgage planning engagement, the client should be given a document to sign off on signifying that the engagement has concluded.

Chapter 9

A Theory That Supports Mortgage Planning
- There's Reasoning Behind The Method -

"A thing moderately good is not so good as it ought to be. Moderation in temper is always a virtue, but moderation in principle is always a vice.

- Thomas Paine –
"The Rights of Man" 1792

Financial planning is criticized by academics because it has no theoretical underpinnings (basis or support). However, this is not true with professional mortgage planning. A theory utilized by the MIFSP supports mortgage planning. The theory is referred to as the Mortgage Portfolio™ Theory (MPT). This theory along with the Mortgage Optimization™ Theory, which is mentioned in this book, also form the underpinning of Mortgage Based™ Financial Planning and MO™ Brand Financial Services offered by Mortgagor Financial Representative™ professionals.

The MPT recognizes the special position that a mortgage on the primary residence holds in relation to the other assets in the client's portfolio. While the primary residence is an asset, it is not generally considered a financial asset, but a physical asset. A financial asset is defined as assets in the form of stocks, bonds, certificates of deposit, mutual funds, bank balances, etc., which are generally intangible in nature.

As stated previously, a mortgaged home represents a trichotomy by commonly being viewed as an investment, a place of shelter (a physical asset) and a financial liability. Historically, there have been few ways, outside of selling the property, to take advantage of the equity buildup in a home without adding to the debt buildup on the home. If you are trying to help the client achieve financial independence, you are also concerned with reducing the level of debt obligations that have to be serviced from current cash flow in order to create the greatest level of financial freedom.

"There are no real get rich quick schemes that actually work".

This was Merrill Lynch advice from 1959 as it appeared in the Houston Chronicle.

As previously stated, census information shows that the home is the primary store of wealth for most people.[17] Consequently, MPT is concerned with the direction the average American's wealth is headed when consumers are lead to use and abuse the equity buildup in their homes. If we accept the census information that the home is most people's greatest store of wealth, then in achieving financial independence, logic would say that it is incumbent upon the average person to protect, preserve and grow the equity in their home. This is one of the benefits in applying the MPT.

According to data from the Federal Reserve Board, Census Bureau and the National Association of Realtors®, in 2001 almost all homeowners (97%) had some equity and the median homeowner had just under $70,000 in home equity. The 2006 annual report, *The State of the Nation's Housing*, released by the Joint Center for Housing Studies of Harvard University, states "…Even with the massive cash-outs over the past several years, home equity still amounts to about 56 percent of the aggregate value of primary residences. At last measure in 2004, escalating home prices had shored up the wealth of most homeowners, with 94 percent having equity of 10 percent or more and 87 percent having equity of 20 percent or more. Only three percent of homeowners had equity stakes of less than five percent… Among those under age 40 with incomes in the $20,000–50,000 range, owners have ten times the median net wealth of renters. Fully half of their $45,640 net wealth is in the form of home equity. Among households in their 40s and 50s with incomes in that same range, the discrepancy is even bigger—$88,000 versus $6,430—with home equity again contributing half of owners' wealth."[18] (The Joint Center for Housing Studies of Harvard University investigates, evaluates and reports on emerging housing issues and community development policies.)

However, instead of using it as one of the last tax-free havens of wealth accumulation, consumers continue to use it as a put and take account. They put money into it (through mortgage payments, maintenance and improvements), and then they take money out of it (through home equity lines of credit, cash-out refinancing and second or third mortgages). Some homeowners find themselves relying on the appreciation of their homes just to meet ordinary expenses.

Changes in the Tax Code in 1986 to allow taxpayers to deduct the interest for consumer loans only if the loan is secured by the home seem to have sent consumers the message that borrowing against home equity is sound economic and financial planning. However, this kind of thinking actually dwindles the wealth and security of millions of American families.

Whether your client already has a home, is contemplating buying a new home, and/or even if it is their first home, they have a chosen lifestyle in mind. The MPT focuses on the client's ability to sustain their chosen lifestyle, a lifestyle within their means. Your clients determine the standard of living that's most suitable for them and they alone (barring an inheritance, etc.) determine the amount of work and effort they are willing to put forth to sustain it.

Mortgage Portfolio™ Theory (MPT) expands consideration of the residential mortgage beyond being a means to finance the purchase of a home or as a way to take advantage of one of the last great tax deductions. By combining mortgage planning principles (the primary principal is recognizing the unique position of each individual client) and the mortgage planning process (six step process) with investment planning techniques and concepts that have been synthesized to mortgages, MPT enables practitioners and consumers alike to consistently make intelligent mortgage management decisions in line with their long and short-term financial and life goals.

MPT (also called mortgage portfolio management theory or modern mortgage portfolio theory) is an enlightened modern mortgage or investment management decision approach that permits a mortgagor to classify, estimate, and control both the kind and amount of risk and return they earn on discretionary dollars that could be earmarked for their mortgage.

In implementing MPT, consumers are encouraged to apply a cognitive process to the determination of how best to utilize those funds. According to MPT, prepaying the mortgage should be viewed just as favorably as any investment in a portfolio if not more favorably.

Like traditional portfolio theory (PT), MPT recognizes the risk return relationship of investments and operates with the assumption that investors should be compensated for assuming risk. MPT helps you to recognize the risk return relationship of the mortgage and builds upon the belief that mortgagors should be compensated for assuming risk, and that they become more fully cognizant of the types of risk they are taking. Awareness of the MPT encourages mortgagors to demand or insist on complete disclosure of all known or expected risks and costs of alternative suggestions to prepaying the mortgage.

The Mortgage Portfolio Theory states:

> **A mortgage free home is a defensive position in any portfolio, and because mortgage financing may be used as a means of financing more than just the acquisition or improvement of the associated property, homeowners may unwittingly take more risk, at far greater expense, and a much lower return than necessary in the pursuit of their financial goals not realizing that prepaying the mortgage either systematically or in a lump sum should be viewed just as favorably as any investment in the portfolio, and the higher the percentage of income from salaries and wages that goes towards meeting housing expenses, the more significant the need to establish a defensive portfolio position and to properly define and assess comparable risk/return differentials.**

As simple as the theory sounds, its development was the result of layers of research and analysis, and its application will have profound effects for the homeowner, the investment industry and the economy. MPT encourages individuals to learn how to properly compare their mortgage options, including how to compare any investment under consideration to prepaying the mortgage with the realization that in the age of "reality everything" the mortgage is no different.

MPT recognizes that (1) a mortgage is not an investment (unless you are the mortgagee), but a debt; (2) paying off the mortgage is totally investment risk free; (3) there is no such thing as a free lunch. We are charged interest for the use of other people's money. The more time we take to pay the money back, the more money it costs us; (4) most mortgages require payment on a monthly basis. Thus any comparable investment should be capable of yielding sufficient income to service the mortgage with the same level or degree of certainty; and number (5) builds upon the previous four and employs a twist on another school of thought regarding stock analysis that is liked very little by those on Wall Street - the Random Walk Theory. The Random Walk Theory was reportedly first espoused in 1900 by a French mathematician, Louis Bachelier, who claimed that stock prices reflect reactions to information coming to the market in a random fashion, such that they are no more predictable than the walking pattern of a drunk. The theory was made popular again in the 1970's by Burton Malkiel in his book, *A RANDOM WALK DOWN WALL STREET*, which claims that both technical and fundamental analysis are basically a waste of time and are still unproven in out performing the markets. He suggests that individuals shouldn't try to time the market, but if they invest, they should employ a buy and hold strategy.

The MPT's twist is this - most of the major stock market theories are statistically based and basically compare and contrast the statistical relationship among classes or even individual securities, or consist of textbook theories built around an ideal model with limited "real world or real life application(s)" and questionable outcomes and simulations. The only statistics in the MPT document the statistical and actual financial foibles of millions of everyday people. MPT is not a statistically based hypothetical fiction, but rather a flexible practical experiential and reality based theory, with a focus on the individual client's "real life" relationship with money and the creation of contractually predictable outcomes. When applied, it significantly reduces the risk commonly associated with the pursuit of life goals. The benefits of homeownership are realized when employing a buy and hold mentality as opposed to a trading mentality and practice.

However, MPT doesn't stop there. By focusing the analysis on the characteristics of the individual residential mortgage and mortgagor, fundamental and technical analysis in hand, MPT allows for the analysis of any other financial assets in the client's or mortgagor's portfolio and enables the mortgagor to make better side-by-side mortgage comparisons and management decisions.

As an investor, a consumer may have as their investment objectives, preservation of capital, liquidity, current income, growth of capital, total return (growth and income), portfolio diversification and asset allocation, among others. However, as a mortgagor, a consumer may generally desire to create, grow and preserve the equity in their home and to ultimately eliminate the debt.

It may be puzzling that a mortgage should be considered part of the portfolio of assets. Actually, it's the lack of a mortgage that we are striving for if the goal is financial independence. Usually once consumers obtain a mortgage it becomes something that's put on the back burner until prompted to refinance for some reason. However, what the MPT suggests is that the consumer take an active role in monitoring and managing their mortgage. Actively monitoring the mortgage will make the consumer more aware of opportunities to optimize its efficiency during the time that they have it.

The defensive portfolio position, put forth under the MPT will likely result in the early elimination of the mortgage, which depending on the consumer's age, could take place prior to retirement. If so, this would drastically reduce the amount of dollars needed at retirement. Being that the mortgage could represent a significant portion of the client's income, the MPT provides a defensive position against uncertainties that could pose obstacles in the path to financial independence.

The MPT is founded on the principle that once the consumer recognizes the defensive position of their mortgage and how it fits into their total or overall portfolio, the consumer will take positive steps to create, grow, protect and preserve the equity in their home before subjecting themselves to risks in the investment market place. This defensive position is a solid backdrop to the lack of guarantees in the investment market.

If the client's goal is to achieve financial independence, MPT suggests that you help the client to determine to what extent a mortgage free home should be a defensive part of that portfolio. Part of the strategy for achieving financial independence will be to develop a course of action to reduce and ultimately eliminate the mortgage. MPT recognizes the general long-term position of a mortgage in the consumer's expanded portfolio structure and thus acknowledges the need to manage and monitor the mortgage like all other components making up the expanded portfolio.

MPT promotes a plan to prepay the mortgage as a defensive portfolio position because with a paid for home your client is provided another layer of financial insurance. They have reduced their need to continue earning at the same level. They are better able to weather any economic storm. A mortgage free home is an excellent hedge against inflation, a down turn in the investment market, and an unexpected loss of income. The basic idea is the lesser the debts the lesser the concerns over income and the lower the actual income needed.

Some argue as reasons for consumers to not prepay the mortgage, the potential for declining property values due to neighborhood changes, lack of liquidity, and/or that a home equity line is the only way to free up cash when necessary. Let's look more closely at these kinds of arguments. First, the mortgage must be paid regardless of what happens to property values. The lender does not reduce the outstanding balance of the mortgage to match the declining value of the house and the consumer can't just walk away from the mortgage (and keep the house) because the value of the property declines.

Second, if the consumer is facing the potential for declining property value, the best thing to do is to pay as little for the property as possible. Being that the mortgage is already in place, the consumer can do one of two things, sell the house or pay off the mortgage. Obviously, if the house can be sold, the declining property value becomes someone else's problem. If the mortgage is paid off early, the interest cost is reduced. The longer the mortgage is in place, the more it costs to have it. By prolonging the term of the mortgage, the total amount paid for the house increases.

Also, if there is concern about the potential for declining property values, then that is good reason not to access the equity in the home via a home equity line. Increasing the mortgages against the property only exacerbates the problem. Consumers may find themselves trapped with a house that they have to pay to get out of. So unless your client's strategy is to pull as much equity out of the home as possible before the values start to decline and then stay in the home until there is a reversal or foreclosure, then it's a good idea to maintain the flexibility that a healthy equity position provides.

Some homeowners have pulled so much equity out of their homes that there is no room to pay real estate sales commissions when they go to sell their homes. They may also find that they have diminished their ability to compete in the sales market. The mortgage balance is at or above the appraised value and/or market value. With no cash reserves, the homeowners may find themselves stuck in a home that no longer suits their needs because they just can't afford to sell.

To satisfy future liquidity concerns, in addition to emergency funds that should be set aside to cover at least three to six months of expenses, after the mortgage has been paid off, funds once used to make the mortgage payment are then freed up for savings or to make other investments.

Let's try to create an apple-to-apple comparison of an investment to prepaying the mortgage by using the following scenario:

A fifty-five year old comes into a $75,000 inheritance and can afford to payoff the mortgage on his townhouse of $69,000. The mortgage has an interest rate of 6 5/8% fixed and a 20-year term.

The question is should he use the money to pay off his mortgage?

Being that the mortgage is a real debt with a real payment and a real due date, its existence cannot be ignored. If the funds are not being used to prepay the mortgage, then the funds should be invested such that it produces funds to cover the monthly cost of the mortgage.

There are two ways this can be done. First, if the investment only produces a rate of return, then he has to sell his investment and realize a gain such that he can produce the funds required to pay the mortgage.

He has to do this continuously, reinvest and sell at a gain each and every month in order to produce the funds needed to make the mortgage payment until the mortgage is satisfied. Of course, there are costs and risks associated with making these investments monthly, which make it highly impractical and unlikely to produce the desired result.

Alternatively, the funds could be invested such that they produce a yield (monthly income) in addition to a return upon the sale. The dilemma is to find an investment that produces a yield sufficient enough to make the monthly mortgage payment. The amount of funds necessary to produce a sufficient yield may far exceed the amount of funds available for the investment.

For example, if we assume that the yield on a bond is 5%, then it would require an investment of $126,000 (almost twice the mortgage balance) in order to produce a monthly yield of $525, which would be sufficient enough to make the mortgage payment in the above example.

So, the first question to ask when comparing an investment to prepaying a mortgage is:

> Does the investment produce a yield, which can be used to make the monthly mortgage payment while your client is waiting to sell the investment and get that rate of return?

If the investment does not produce a monthly yield, then the investment hasn't gotten your client any closer to financial independence because they still have to work in order to pay the mortgage.

If the investment produces a yield, the question is, given current yields, how much money must your client have invested in order to produce a monthly amount sufficient enough to make the mortgage payment?

If the amount required to pay the mortgage is more than the amount available, then your client has got to work to produce enough funds to fill the gap between the yield and the mortgage payment.

When your client is being directed toward investments and away from prepaying the mortgage, you shouldn't let your client lose sight of the realities of an existing mortgage.

It may go against the grain of everything you've ever heard about investing. Even financial experts appear timid about being definitive when it comes to the financial benefits of paying off a mortgage. It's as though they believe that they are recommending that consumers give away money.

In reality, it's just the opposite. First recognize that the mortgage must be paid. The consumer has a contractual obligation to do so. The only way to eliminate the mortgage is to pay if off.

Obtaining a residential mortgage is one of the first major adult financial decisions made by most people. After that, mortgage decisions of one kind or another follow most people for the next thirty years or more. It's in recognition of the significance of the mortgage that MPT infuses a low risk, no cost option into the consumers' financial planning and investment strategy.

Summary

One of the academic criticisms of financial planning is that it has no theoretical underpinnings. Mortgage planning, however, is supported by both the Mortgage Portfolio™ Theory and the Mortgage Optimization™ Theory. These theories support the idea that a mortgage should be planned for just like any other aspect of your finances. By combining mortgage planning principles and the mortgage planning process (six step process) with investment planning techniques and concepts that have been synthesized to mortgages, MPT enables practitioners and consumers alike to consistently make intelligent mortgage management decisions in line with their long and short-term financial and life goals.

MPT expands consideration of the residential mortgage beyond being a means to finance the purchase of a home or as a way to take advantage of one of the last great tax deductions. The theory suggests, among other things, that the consumer take an active role in monitoring and managing their mortgage such that he or she is more aware of opportunities to optimize its efficiency during the time that they have it and to realize when it's outlived its usefulness. One of your goals as a mortgage planner should be to help your client do just that.

Chapter 10

A Uniform Process Comes Info Focus - We're All On The Same Page –

"If we can implant in our people the Christian virtues which we sum up in the word character, and, at the same time, give them a knowledge of the line which should be drawn between voluntary action and governmental compulsion in a democracy, and of what can be accomplished within the stern laws of economics, we will enable them to retain their freedom, and at the same time, make them worthy to be free."

- Winthrop Williams Aldrich -

As was stated in Chapter 1, use of standardized processes and concepts should enable professional mortgage planners to not only distinguish themselves in the market place, but should also help manage consumer expectations and start all QMP™ professionals on the same page. In other words, we recommended that certain procedures, processes, and practices be followed that will result in providing certain basic information to the client. Uniformity in these areas will enable QMP™ professionals and their clients to know where (and how) to start the mortgage planning engagement, who and what's involved, and when the engagement is over. If you haven't noticed by now, the six steps put forth in Chapters 2 through 8 satisfy this recommendation.

In Chapters 2, the first step of the mortgage planning process is to **establish a relationship** with the client, however, we began with knowing yourself well enough that you can identify what you bring to the mortgage planning relationship. The second step, identified in Chapter 3, is to **gather qualitative and quantitative data** from the client so that you can develop the mortgage plan. Chapter 5 describes step three, **data analysis and evaluation**. In Chapter 6, we identified step four, **plan development**. Step five is **plan implementation**, which was explained in Chapter 7. The last step of the mortgage planning process is **monitoring** as explained in Chapter 8.

What should not be surprising is that these six steps mirror the six-step financial planning process generally recognized in the financial services industry. However, the application of the steps is modified to fit the mortgage planning engagement. If you are in sales, then you may also realize that the six-steps do not differ much from the traditional sales cycle.

How can you tell the difference between a salesperson, a financial planner and a medical doctor in relation to the sales cycle? The difference is not in the steps it's in how the steps are applied.

Sales Process	Sales Person	Financial Planner	Medical Doctor
Step I	May make an Introduction	Will Define Relationship	Makes an Introduction
Step II	May Be Confidence Inspiring	Will Gather Client Data	Collects "Patient" Data – Uncover Interest & Needs
Step III	May Expand the Prospects Self Regard	Will Analyze & Evaluate Client Financial Status	Analyze & Evaluate Patient's Health Status
Step IV	May Uncover Interests & Needs	Will Developing and Presenting Financial Planning Recommendations and/or Alternatives	Develops and Presents Medical "Prescription", and/or Alternatives
Step V	May Make it Easy for Prospect to Decide	May Implementing the Financial Planning Recommendations	Implements the Prescription
Step VI	May Maintain Contact	May Monitor Financial Planning Recommendations	Monitors situation

Source: *The ABCs of Mortgaged Based Financial Planning*

In looking at the table above and thinking about the sales cycle, what revelations, if any, come to mind about what they may share in common and what differentiates them? The commonality is that they all use something very similar to a six-step process or the sales cycle in doing their jobs. The difference is in the professional thinking and reasoning skills used in relation to how they spend their day.

The sales process is not all that different in each one of the occupations. The salesperson is said to be transaction oriented and may do a number of things to ensure a fit between the client's needs, goals, objectives, and the products or services they offer. When you consider the role of the medical doctor, there are a number of other differences that you may have already noted about the three examples above. Several items that may immediately come to mind for instance are the fact that these are three distinct career paths; there is a difference in skills and knowledge required for each pursuit.

Selling is an acquired skill, just like a medical doctor's bedside manner. While bedside manner may differ significantly between doctors, a common factor is that the doctor can't cure what he doesn't know is ailing you and neither can the financial planner. Selling is not just a matter of luck, but a combination of personal characteristics, acquired skills, and organizational characteristics. For each of the professions, professional improvement may come from a desire to improve and grow his or her business.

The complexity of the process is not what's at issue here, it's the uniform application of that process by those in the mortgage planning profession that counts most when it comes to setting a honorable standard and garnering consumer trust and respect. Mortgage planning has to be associated with high ethical standards and competent practitioners in order to survive and thrive as a financial services specialty. It is up to qualified mortgage planners to recognize the need for competence and for ethical standards, to accept those standards, and to live up to them.

There are over 100 million households including those households that are hoping to become first time homebuyers. A unique opportunity exists for the mortgage planning professional to move to the forefront on the consumers' financial planning agenda and to catapult mortgage planning into a highly sort after worthwhile specialty satisfying the consumers' need for professional independent mortgage advice and a connection between mortgage decisions and their overall financial goals and objectives. In its truest form, mortgage planning can do anything from improving the quality of service provided by mortgage originators to becoming a viable stand-alone profession.

The precarious position of many homeowners as it relates to their mortgage demonstrates an obvious need for mortgage planning. In a speech given by Daniel H. Mudd, President and CEO, Fannie Mae before the National Association of Realtors Regional Summit on Housing Opportunities on April 24, 2006, he stated, "…By the year 2020, 18 percent of Americans will be Hispanic. The African American population will grow by 19 percent. The Asian population will grow by 44 percent. We'll see an influx of people from nations that most educated Americans can't place on a map. Quite often, these families have the least understanding about the mortgage process. So we and our lending partners need to make sure they get the safest, cheapest, best mortgage products and prices for which we can qualify them. These folks are the future of real estate in our area…"[19]

Along with serving as a source of independent mortgage advice, by way of mortgage planning you can help mortgagors devise a no cost low risk way of preparing for retirement. Being that the home is the largest expense for the average person, mortgage planning that ultimately results in a paid for home significantly relieves the strain on retirement income such that concerns about the insecurity of social security, poor saving habits or poorly performing investments are alleviated. If there ever comes an overwhelming need to access equity in a paid for house, the introduction of reverse mortgages provides homeowners a way to access the equity in their homes without incurring monthly payments and risking loss of the property. Leaving piece of mind in tact.

Mortgage planning brings hope for a risk free and worry free way to reach financial freedom to those who believe a few dollars can't go a long way, and for those who think that high risks are the only way to achieve a worthwhile return. Without a doubt, the benefits of mortgage planning have the potential to change the spending and investing habits of millions of homeowners. Being that the home is the greatest store of wealth for most Americans, rather than exploiting that fact QMP™ professionals and MFR™ professionals can help Americans preserve and grow their wealth by offering a better way.

Those who now practice as mortgage planners, those who now feel inspired to become Qualified Mortgage Planner™ professionals or Mortgage Financial Representative™ professional, and those consumers who now have a greater understanding of the benefits of mortgage planning should see the far-reaching possibilities of how this financial specialty can make a valuable contribution to society and to protecting the financial strength of the American family.

Summary

Uniformity in the process used for mortgage planning will enable mortgage planners and their clients to know where (and how) to start the mortgage planning engagement, who and what's involved, and when the engagement is over. Use of a standardized process and concepts should enable professional mortgage planners to not only distinguish themselves in the market place, but should also help manage consumer expectations and start all mortgage planners on the same page.

The fundamental steps in the mortgage planning process are no different from the six steps of the financial planning process or the steps in the traditional sales cycle. The differences lie in the professional thinking and reasoning skills used and in how the steps are applied.

As a QMP™ professional, you are providing consumers a professional service unmatched by any other financial services professional in the country and you can help consumers determine the issue of mortgage suitability on a level as yet unsurpassed. When it comes to mortgages, as a QMP™ professional, there is always a role for you whether it's before, during and/or after the mortgage transaction. The goal of this book is to help prepare you to accept those roles.

Glossary of Terms

Associate, Residential Mortgage Planner™ Professional - a person who meets the experience and educations requirements for conferment and who has completed the Mortgage Based™ Financial Planning educational program at the Mortgage Institute of Financial Services Professionals. Also see Mortgagor Financial Representative™ Professional.

Fiduciary - a person who owes to another the duties of good faith, trust, confidence, and candor. One who must exercise a high standard of care in managing another's property or money.

Financial Planning Process - a client centered process of examining a client's personal situation, financial resources, financial objectives and financial problems to develop a an impartial integrated plan approved by the client to solve the client's problems and meet the client's objectives and monitored on a regular basis so that corrective action can be taken to assure that plan performance meets plan projections.

Good Faith Estimate – a good faith estimate of the settlement cost the borrower is likely to incur at closing.

Letter of Engagement - a written agreement between a consumer and a financial services professional listing the type of services to be provided, the responsibilities and relationship of the parties, the time frame for delivery of the service and when the fee to be paid is considered earned. In an MFR™ engagement, it explains in simple terms the services to be performed, the cost for the services rendered, how and when the costs are to be paid, and the fiduciary relationship of the MFR™ professional.

Mortgagee – the lender or the one that holds a mortgage

Mortgage Fundamental™ Analysis - a client centered process that focuses on the client's financial position and goals and the appropriate matching of the two so as to answer fundamental questions such as: is a mortgage necessary; and if a mortgage is necessary, whether it's due to objective or subjective reasoning; and if a mortgage exists, whether it's priced at, below or at a premium to the existing mortgage market.

Mortgage Pre-payment Equivalent Yield™ - is a calculation based on comparing the taxpayer's financial situation with and without a mortgage relative to a specific property to one or more alternative investment options of varying amounts up to and including an amount equal to the payoff of the existing or proposed mortgage balance. It further illustrates which direction the financial benefits flow between investing or prepaying the mortgage by comparing any loss or gain in tax benefits, any loss or gain in actual cash flow between the options, and recognizing the tax free rental value of the property. The result of this calculation is the mortgage pre-payment equivalent yield™ (MPEY). The MPEY™ is a value that can be used in comparing prepaying the mortgage to the projected rates of return of any investment.

Mortgage Mission™ Statement – a statement that describes the financial objectives of the mortgage and the rationale for the mortgage

Mortgage Optimization™ Theory – a holistic theory based on the interplay of principles and concepts from law, finance, economics, income taxation, financial planning and mortgages. The theory is based on the premise that the mortgage can be designed to maximize the benefits of having it while it's needed, to minimize the costs while it's in place, and to recognize when it's surpassed its optimal utility.

Mortgage Portfolio™ Theory – a theory based on the premise that having a paid for home is a defensive portfolio position against uncertainties that could pose obstacles in the path to reaching core financial objectives such as financial independence, and that actively monitoring the mortgage will make the client more aware of opportunities to optimize its efficiency during the time that they have the mortgage

Mortgage Ratio Analysis™ - examines the client's ratios beyond the traditional housing ratios of loan to value, debt to income, housing costs to income and reserves. The analysis examines the ratio of housing expense relative to income sources (unearned, dividend and interest income), reserves relative to qualified, non-qualified accounts and emergency reserves, and the mortgage balance relative to financial and non-financial asset classes.

Mortgage Risk Analysis™ - identifies and examines the types of risk (investment, management, timing, principal, tax, liquidity, inflation and interest rate risk) taken by the client when discretionary funds are allocated to alternative uses rather than being applied to the mortgage balance

Mortgage Strategy & Investment Policy™ Statement – a statement that describes with specificity the tactics or methods to be employed to maximize the benefits of having a mortgage while simultaneously minimizing the total present and future costs of having a mortgage

Mortgage Tax Benefit - is calculated on an individual basis and identifies the actual dollar benefit of having a mortgage in place for any given scenario (prospective, current or historical) experienced by the client. The calculation is the sum of the qualified home deductions less the standard deduction or itemized deductions less the mortgage interest multiplied by the mortgagor's marginal tax rate. This value captures the tax benefits associated with the qualified home.

Mortgage Tax Benefit™ Analysis - is a two-part calculation whereby the advisor calculates the mortgage tax benefit and then the mortgage tax ratio. The mortgage tax benefit is the sum of the qualified home deductions less the standard deduction multiplied by the marginal tax rate. This value captures the tax benefits associated with the qualified home. The mortgage tax ratio is calculated by dividing the mortgage tax benefit by gross income.

Mortgage Technical™ Analysis - a financial analysis that is concerned with the examination of the client's fundamental data (personal and property characteristics) on an objective basis. This analysis is used to determine if an existing or proposed mortgage is less expensive or more expensive than another or to make comparisons to what is readily available in the contemporaneous marketplace given considerations such as: the mortgage term, rate, expected closing costs, loan to value, debt to income, credit score, payback period, etc.

Mortgagor – the borrower or homeowner, the one that mortgages the property

Mortgagor Financial Representative™ Professional – individuals licensed by the MIFSP to provide consumers independent mortgage advisory services before, during and/or after the mortgage transaction. The MFR™ professional acts as a fiduciary and provides standalone advice independent of a mortgage transaction

Qualified Mortgage Planner™ Professional – a person who meets the requirements to be included as a listee in the national registry sponsored by the National Association of Independent Mortgage Service Providers, a division of the Mortgage Institute for Financial Services Professionals.

Residential Mortgage Planner™ Professional - a person who meets the experience and educations requirements for conferment and who has completed the Mortgage Based™ Financial Planning educational program at the Mortgage Institute of Financial Services Professionals. Also see Mortgagor Financial Representative™ Professional.

Index

N

O

P

Q

R

S

Footnotes:

---

[1] Consumer Federation of America. (2006) Press Release Dated May 24, 2006. Retrieved from http://www.consumerfed.org/pdfs/Exotic_Toxic_Mortgage_Release052406.pdf

[2] U.S. Department of Labor, Bureau of Labor Statistics. *Consumer Expenditure Survey,*2002.

[3] Joint Center for Housing Studies at Harvard University. (2006) *The State of the Nation's Housing:2006.* Retrieved from: http://www.jchs.harvard.edu/publications/markets/son2006/son2006_bw.pdf

[4] Remarks by Mary L. Schapiro, Vice Chairman, NASD President, Regulatory Policy & Oversight on August 4, 2006 at the 2006 Annual Meeting of the Certified Financial Planner Board of Standards, Inc. Retrieved from: http://www.nasd.com/PressRoom/SpeechesTestimony/MaryL.Schapiro/NASDW_017096

[5] Elmerick, Stephanie A., Montalto, Catherine P., Fox, Jonathan J. (2002). Use of financial planners by U.S. households, *Financial Services Review*, 11, 217-231.

[6] National Association of Securities Dealers. (2004). Press release dated March 15, 2004. Retrieved from http://www.nasd.com/PressRoom/NewsReleases/2004NewsReleases/NASDW_002844

[7] National Association of Realtors®. (2006). Press release dated January 17, 2006. Home buyer & seller survey shows rising use of Internet, reliance on agents.

[8] National Association of Realtors®. (2006). Median sales price of existing single-family homes for metropolitan areas. Retrieved from www.realtor.org/research.nsf/pages/metroprice.

[9] Realtytrac. (2006) National foreclosures remain elevated in September, according to Realtytrac report. RISMEDIA, October 12, 2006. Retrieved from http://www.rismedia.com/index.php/article/articleview/16720/1/1/

[10] RISMedia. (2006) Home prices finally hit wall. RISMedia, September 27, 2006. Retrieved from http://www.rismedia.com/index.php/article/articleview/16067/1/1

[11] National Association of Mortgage Brokers (2006) Choose a NAMB certified mortgage broker when financing your home. Retrieved from http://www.namb.org/namb/Current_Designees.asp?SnID=1247515688

[12] Johnson & Johnson, (2006) Our Credo. Retrieved from http://www.jnj.com/our_company/our_credo/index.htm

[13] Leider, Richard J., (1985) *The Power of Purpose 1st Edition,* pg viii

[14] Sestina, John. (2001*). Fee-Only Financial Planning,* pg 6.

[15] Spitzer, John J., Singh, Sandeep., (2004). The pay-down or prepayment of a home mortgage, *Journal of Financial services Professionals,* November 2004. A superior competing investment, in our opinion, is a default-free annuity whose present value (after accounting for tax cash flows discounted at the post tax mortgage rate) exceeds the nominal value of the mortgage.

[16] Kelvin, Jeffrey B., Ruckstuhl, William J., (1990). *Vol.1Financial Planning Applications 9th Edition.*

[17] U.S. Census Bureau

[18] Joint Center for Housing Studies at Harvard University. (2006) *The State of the Nation's Housing: 2006* Retrieved From http://www.jchs.harvard.edu/publications/markets/son2006/son2006_bw.pdf

[19] Fannie Mae. (2006). Remarks prepared for delivery by Daniel H. Mudd, President & CEO on April 24, 2006 at the NAR Regional Summit on Housing Opportunities Vienna, Virginia., Retrieved from http://www.fanniemae.com/media/speeches/speech.jhtml?repID=/media/speeches/2006/speech_259.xml&p=Media&s=Executive+Speeches&counter=8

Made in United States
Orlando, FL
04 November 2026

90200296R00125